Born and raised on an island off the coast of Norway, Marie Forsberg grew up learning the arts of gardening, foraging, and cooking from her talented and resourceful mother. Post-university, she traveled the world as a photographer, discovering new ingredients and dishes wherever she went. On a trip to London, she ended up falling in love with the English countryside. Inspired by the rolling meadows and charming villages, she decided to make a small thatched cottage her home. The wealth of produce from local markets and farms led her to reconnect with the culinary roots of her upbringing, creating a cooking style of her own in the process. Marie began her popular blog, *The Cottage Kitchen*, to chronicle her new life.

In her debut cookbook, Marie shares seasonal recipes and sumptuous photography—occasionally featuring Mr. Whiskey, her English Pointer and constant companion—that will transport any food lover and Anglophile to the country lanes and quaint towns of England.

THE
COTTAGE
KITCHEN

COZY COOKING IN THE
ENGLISH COUNTRYSIDE

MARTE MARIE FORSBERG

CLARKSON POTTER/PUBLISHERS

New York

CLARKSON POTTER is a trademark and
POTTER with colophon is a registered
trademark of Penguin Random House LLC.

Library of Congress Cataloging-in-
Publication Data
Names: Forsberg, Marte Marie, author. |
    Forsberg, Marte Marie, photographer.
Title: The cottage kitchen : cozy cooking in
    the English countryside / Marte Marie
    Forsberg ; photographs by Marte Marie
    Forsberg.
Description: First edition. | New York :
    Clarkson Potter/Publishers, [2017] |
    Includes index.
Identifiers: LCCN 2016056229 | ISBN
    9780451495761 (hc) | ISBN 9780451495778
    (eISBN)
Subjects: LCSH: Cooking, English. | Seasonal
    cooking. | Cooking—England. | LCGFT:
    Cookbooks.

Classification: LCC TX717 .F57 2017 | DDC
    641.5942—dc23 LC record available at
    https://lccn.loc.gov/2016056229

ISBN 978-0-451-49576-1
Ebook 978-0-451-49577-8

Printed in China

Cover and book design by Marysarah Quinn

Cover and interior photographs by Marte
Marie Forsberg

10 9 8 7 6 5 4 3 2 1

First Edition

To Yvonne and Oddvar Forsberg,

my beloved parents,

whose unwavering love, support, and friendship

I cherish with all my heart.

CONTENTS

INTRODUCTION

I T TAKES LESS THAN TWO HOURS by train to travel from the bustling city of London to my English cottage that's tucked away on the border between two shires, Dorset and Wilshire. On a cold and foggy November afternoon a few years ago, I boarded that train for the first time, and eagerly looked out the windows as we steadily made our way through the cultivated English landscape of rolling hills and groomed old estates. Over streams and rivers we went, bending back and forth underneath brick bridges and passing stone cottages that dotted the edges of narrow countryside lanes. A taxi picked me up at the other end. I pressed my nose up against the window, trying to peer through the fog that seemed to grow thicker and thicker the higher we went. As the driver easily navigated what seemed like impossibly narrow streets that wound through the little town situated on the top of a Saxon hill, my excited nerves were calmed ever so slightly. You see, I was on my way to see my love for the very first time, and I felt a bit nervous.

We hadn't yet met, but I knew it was love at first sight—or at least, at first photograph. The night before, I had tossed and turned for hours, blaming my restlessness on the full moon that lit up the guest bedroom I was staying in like it was daytime, all the while trying to hold back tears. I failed more times than not, soaking my pillow with tears of feeling lost in this big world. I'd been struggling to find my voice, a direction, and a home.

After years of travels and living abroad, I had moved back to my home country, Norway. I had thought, perhaps naively so, that I was going home, which of course I was in a way. I had returned to my childhood roots, but when I unpacked my suitcase after more than twelve years of living in various places around the world, a result of my work and studies, all I could feel was that I was lost. The woman I'd become after all these years was not marinating in homecoming bliss, that comforting feeling of knowing you belong. Rather, I was sad to acknowledge that all those years had changed me, leaving me with a deep gratitude and love for where I was born, while acknowledging that the woman I'd become might belong somewhere else.

So there I was spending the night in a bed-and-breakfast in England, between a job shooting a campaign for an American fashion brand and meetings in London, crying big wet tears of not knowing where I belonged in this world. "Where do I go from here?" I desperately wanted to type into the search box on the Internet. So I did, or nearly did. I wiped my eyes clear of salty tears, opened a blank search page on my mobile phone, and typed, "Houses for rent in England."

Little did I know how those very words would change my life forever.

Twelve pages in, I fell in love. With a house.

It was love at first sight, and I knew, inexplicably, that this was my future home. I looked at the photo of the white thatched cottage with a tiny garden surrounded by a white picket fence over and over. This cottage was my home—I could feel it—and it really didn't matter where it was located. As far as I was concerned, I already lived there anyway. In a smaller text underneath the photo, the name of the town was written. *Shaftesbury*, it read, and I sounded it out in the dark moonlit room, as if I was learning to pronounce a word for a magical spell for the very first time . . . Shaftesbury . . .

The next day, I was on the train. And it didn't take much persuasion for me to sign on the dotted line. Eagerly, I returned to Norway, only to pack my bags and return to England for a shiny new chapter— to my new home.

EVERY CHIMNEY OF THE COTTAGES in my new hometown bellowed out smoke on a daily basis that first winter, indicating a cozy fire crackling away inside, warming its inhabitants with a steady glow. Mine had one too. In the center of the living room—with its low ceiling of dark wood beams—there was a big old stone fireplace with a wonky wooden lintel piece that looked like it had been there ever since the cottage was built hundreds of years ago. The wood was darkened by time and dotted with tiny holes where woodworm had feasted over the years. The cottage had a hobbit-like entrance with a white stable door, a straw roof, a tiny kitchen, and a small yet inviting bathtub, just large enough for me to either submerge my legs or back, but never both at the same time. I filled the shed at the back of the garden with wood, storing up for the long winter ahead, and began exploring my new hometown.

I learned quickly that, although Norway has longer and colder winters than England, there's nothing more bone-chillingly cold than the latter. During the first winter in my new home, freezing winds made a mess of my wavy blond hair and pinched my pale cheeks pink. I stuffed my rubber wellies with knitted woolen socks to stay warm, and explored the nearby hills via the muddy paths and narrow countryside lanes. Despite being wrapped in oversized wool coats, knitted mittens, and a fluffy warm scarf, nothing seemed to keep the humid cold from penetrating the many winter layers I had on. I felt exposed.

I was no stranger to setting up a new camp or living abroad. Ever since the age of fifteen, I'd spent summers living in Switzerland to learn Swiss German. I moved to Tokyo at the age of seventeen, quickly followed by new adventures in Italy, where I studied fashion design in Milan. When I was twenty, I worked as a flight attendant for Scandinavian Airlines, and lived in the Dominican Republic before moving to Malta for studies. My love for exploring new cultures and languages led me to seek a second degree in Middle Eastern studies at a university in America, where I simultaneously immersed myself in the American way of life. However, this move felt new. It was less about a new adventure, and more about coming home.

"Are you sure you won't be lonely over there in England all by yourself, so far away from friends and family?" my beloved mother asked, after I announced I was moving again. "I'll be fine," I said, brushing off her loving concern. But I knew in my heart I would—of course I would. But here's the thing about when you get that deep feeling of knowing something is right: There's an inexplicable feeling of warmth and calm that guides you in an unexpected direction, and you unwaveringly choose to follow, because you trust, you leap, hoping that all your questions will be answered as you go along. It feels like a pillar of strength is erected inside of you, and even if you know you'll be lonely and that it will be hard—harder than you ever imagined—you also trust that you'll develop all the strength you need as you choose to have faith, both in the journey and, perhaps even more so, in yourself.

THERE'S A FOOD MARKET IN TOWN every Thursday where farmers, florists, cheese- and fish-mongers, and a local baker all set up tables along high street to present baskets and wooden crates filled to the brim with fresh seasonal produce and newly caught seafood. It has supplied my kitchen with wonderful, quality produce from day one. Much as my mother's garden in my childhood home in Norway has faithfully supplied her kitchen with produce through the ever-changing seasons, so did the market in town supply me and my kitchen. Potatoes, rutabaga, and kale fill the wicker baskets during the sleepier months of the year, and during the summer the baskets are heaped with an ever-changing abundance of seasonal fruit and vegetables. Even the town hall doors are open wide to display all the indoor stalls of people wanting to practically give away their gardens' yield.

During that first year, when the artichokes arrived in late June, I leapt with joy and created simple dishes with the spiky green vegetable, reminiscing of my time in Italy. And as the golden chanterelles appeared in late summer, I returned home to the cottage with armfuls of the mushroom, simply throwing them into a sizzling skillet with a gentle sprinkle of salt and pepper and a generous knob of butter, just as my mother used to do. As it turned out, this is when I felt most at home during those first few months in my little English cottage, re-creating nostalgic childhood dishes with produce from the local town market.

I grew up in the countryside, on an island on the outskirts of a fjord in Norway. Being the youngest of four, I spent much time in my mother's company, watching her cook and bake. Saying that I learned to cook on my mother's knee is both true and untrue. I watched her in the kitchen as a child, sitting on the kitchen counter as she prepared our family meals. My job was more that of a supporting actor than the main cast. I cracked eggs, or stirred and kneaded dough, but I was always more excited about the eating part than the preparing part. Impatient by nature, I eagerly anticipated when we would all take a seat around the big oak dining room table, light candles, and enjoy the wonderful dishes that my mother had made. Daily family gatherings of this kind were a steady heartbeat in our home.

As I grew older, the cooking aspect became one of my absolute favorite parts of the day, and a favored part of the meal, when it's me, the kitchen, and endless possibilities ahead, and perhaps a bit of Aretha Franklin or Billie Holiday playing on the radio, cheekily sipping a glass of wine, true Keith Floyd–style. I find so much joy in taking the beautiful goods from the farmers' market and transforming them into delicious bites to savor, and this process and practice has ended up turning my love-at-first-sight cottage into a true home.

This cookbook shares my story of wanderings and perhaps finding myself again after years of travels, and of all the dishes I cooked along the way. The move to the countryside, and finding the cottage, created a base, a safe haven in which to reconnect with my roots, and I discovered what my heart had been yearning for—that sense of belonging that had been so elusive during my travels. All the women in my family share a passion for cooking, creating meals, all of which nod to the different seasons, and have a slight disregard for tradition where the spirit of my culinary roots lies. Many of the dishes in these pages are heavily influenced by my travels, filled with flavors and aromas from these journeys. Others are utterly inspired by what I discover in the English countryside with its delicious local fare. This culinary journey of mine, led by my nose, and becoming a culinary magpie of sorts has allowed me to start a new chapter in my life, in a home much like the one I grew up in, with something always simmering on the stove. And if I can hope for one thing, it is that this cookbook may inspire you, too, to cook more and perhaps rediscover, as I did, the joy of a comforting home-cooked meal, shared with people you love.

winter

"IT'S GOING TO SNOW TONIGHT," MY MOTHER would say, as she turned her nose toward the dark blue sky, inhaling the crisp winter air. I'd look at her in awe; she knew so many things. "How do you know?" I'd eagerly ask. She'd turn to me and point toward the moon. "The moon has a halo around it; can you see it?" she asked, still pointing toward the sky. And then, she said, letting out a delighted sigh, "You can smell it in the air."

The smell of snow is quite distinct, yet hard to describe. It's a crispness in the air, containing little to no perfume, unlike the fresh, "green" aroma after summer rain, or a wet storm in autumn. No, this is different; it smells crisp and blue, if color can have a smell. It marks the beginning of winter, pointing to the long, dark, and moody months ahead. It also marks the countdown to the biggest feast of the year: Christmas.

What cold, snowy winter landscapes may lack in outdoor perfume they certainly make up for in exotic and delicious aromas filling the kitchen this time of the year. In Norway, the lids on glass jars containing spices from far-flung corners of the world are finally popped open. Whole cloves, cardamom pods, and peppercorns—these smells are to me unmistakably Christmas in nature, as are the dark brown cinnamon sticks hanging from our Christmas tree, tied with ruby-red silk ribbons.

On those evenings when my mother would turn her nose up toward the sky, inhaling the first signs of winter, my father would tuck me in at night. I'd lie wide awake with excitement. The smell in the air, the ring around the moon, the arrival of snow—all mark the transition from one season to another, bringing with it a much anticipated culinary change.

After mushroom-hunting and berry-picking season was over, my mother's kitchen didn't turn frugal or bare due to the decline in fresh produce. Winter always felt like a season of feasts, one after another, where familiar produce enjoyed fresh during summer and autumn would now be served pickled, frozen, and made into jam or cordials, and meat would be salted and hung to dry in the pantry. The kitchen entered a season when my mother was rarely seen without an apron on, since there was so much to do before Christmas. Even if snow was imminent, her garden had yet to completely doze off until spring, and still yielded a few persistent vegetables amongst the fallen fruit gathering on the ground alongside frozen leaves. The last apples would be carefully brought inside, wrapped in newspaper, and placed in boxes in the cool basement. "Everything has its use," she'd tell me, pointing toward the rather sad-looking pile of bruised apples in the wicker basket on the kitchen table. "These will make the sweetest jam and jelly," she'd say with a smile. Behind the brown spots and bruised sides, these apples had ripened to perfection, so down into the basement they went, all wrapped up in ink-smudged old newspaper, like little presents from a bygone era.

A clear blue sky and brisk winds dominated my first days and weeks at my cottage in England. It takes time to settle into a new place, a new home, to find a rhythm to let each room of the house introduce itself to you and each nook of the surrounding landscape to become familiar. I began with the kitchen, opening its doors to the garden and exploring the wilted plants, turning over pebbles and imagining what spring would look like here.

I'd wander the quiet streets of my new hometown engulfed in thick winter fog, seemingly deserted. When my fingers and toes got too cold, I'd duck into a wonky tearoom for afternoon tea. I discovered at the top of the hill a house built during the Tudor era, with big old fireplaces, white plaster walls, and those distinct black wooden beams. I felt as if I'd stepped back in time as I poured steaming hot tea from an elegant pot and swirled milk around my cup with a small spoon. Watching the tea and milk marbleize together, I let the warm cup soothe my freezing hands, thinking to myself how easily I might adopt this English afternoon ritual.

Peering through the large bay window from my seat, I imagined what life must have been like here when King Henry VIII ruled England and destroyed the most beautiful abbey, which had crowned the top of the hill in town since AD 888, just a stone's throw away from where I sat. Later, walking past the abbey remains, I caught myself gazing in its direction, imagining how magnificent it must have looked. Towering high above the valley, with views of the sea on a clear day, this abbey—which had been run by women—had been the largest of its kind in northern Europe at the time. Now, all that was left was ruins after King Henry VIII ordered it to be pulled down and for the stones to be sold. Some say you can hear the nuns' angelic voices rising toward the sky at dawn, welcoming the emerging new day with a sacred hymn. Perhaps the women who had joined the convent here hundreds of years ago had made the journey to this hill for similar reasons as I had, to seek refuge and comfort away from the world in a time of need.

"ARE YOU FEELING *ENSOM* OR *ALENE*?" my mother wanted to know one day as we spoke on the phone. I paused, trying to listen to how I felt.

In Norwegian we have these two words, *ensom*, which describes being lonely, and *alene*, which describes being on your own. They are distinctly different words, yet describe two sides of the same thing. She wanted to know which of these described my state the best, the way I was feeling as I began to settle into my home in England. I hesitated as I mulled the two words over.

"Rarely *ensom*," I began. "But I do feel sentimental about being *alene*," I continued.

She paused. "Acknowledge the feeling of *ensom*, but I hope you won't linger in it. It can be soul destroying if one does," she said somberly. "However, being *alene*, or being on your own, is needed for growth, and is an undervalued tool for progress and for finding ourselves amidst the many voices and elements of noise in the world," she added with warmth in her voice. I nodded on the other end of the line, a bit too choked up to utter any words.

I missed her, and I missed my family and friends, even if they came to visit often. Of course this was not the first time I had lived abroad, away from my childhood home in Norway, but it felt different this time around—perhaps because I had this emerging feeling that this was not a visit to another country, but rather an indefinite move.

After our phone call, I paced around the cottage, mulling her words over. Upon catching my reflection in the hallway mirror, I hesitated. "It's going to be all right," I whispered to my own reflection, all choked up. Deep down, in a nook to the right of my heart, I felt this incredible yearning, a longing, after years and years of travels, of gathering experiences, filling me to the brim with inspiration, to finally put my bag down, and begin creating for myself, to create a home.

To reignite my passion for home-cooked meals, the simple, rustic cuisine of my childhood, and to create a home for the woman I'd become.

WINTER IN THE ENGLISH COUNTRYSIDE revolves around hearty food, such as perfectly pink Sunday roast with a side of Yorkshire pudding, bangers and mash, and game—that is consumed more often than not.

Game regularly appeared in the household I grew up in too, sending my father rummaging in the basement for his saws and my mother preparing the kitchen and cleaning the big oak dining room table. A family friend on his way down from the mountains would occasionally pay us a visit in the evenings as the temperature dropped below zero, and he'd place a whole deer or moose on the table. Starting by dividing up the parts, the men in my family would gut and part the beast, while I watched on in awe. Meanwhile, Mum heated pots and pans in the kitchen, browning the liver with a bit of butter as an evening meal for the hardworking men to enjoy.

Game found at the market in my English countryside town of Shaftesbury is thankfully much more manageable, consisting mainly of pheasants, rabbits, partridge, and pigeon. That first winter in England, each week I would try something new, testing out old traditional recipes and making them my own. My pots and pans, never having time to gather dust, looked shinier than ever, and I began to find my own rhythm. My heartbeat had begun to steady, and I felt a tingling excitement for the year ahead as I settled into this new life of mine in the English countryside.

"Come what may," I whispered, to no one in particular.

STARTERS AND SIDES

Foie Gras and Kidney Bruschetta
with Parsley

Fig and Pecan No-Knead Bread

Waldorf Salad

Truffled Yorkshire Pudding
with Onion Gravy

Warm Salmon, Mint,
and Potato Salad

No-Knead Country Loaf

Tarragon Butter Baked Scallops

MAINS

Chorizo Macaroni and Cheese

Norwegian Pork Belly
with Mustard Coleslaw
and Brown Gravy

Norwegian Sweet Rice Cream
Porridge with Cinnamon

Truffled Vegetable
Toad-in-the-Hole

Creamy Fish Soup with Clams

Warming Lamb and
Cabbage Stew

Butter Baked Cod with Saffron
and Parsley Sauce

DESSERTS

My Father's Troll Cream

Saffron and Vanilla Poached Pears

Olga's Caramel Pudding

Norwegian Waffles with
Strawberries and Sour Cream

Crema Catalana

DRINKS AND JAMS

Lemon Curd

Limoncello

Campari Citrus Marmalade

FOIE GRAS AND KIDNEY BRUSCHETTA WITH PARSLEY

Makes 4 bruschetta

During the colder months of the year, I yearn for rustic comfort food that's full of flavor. This delightful little starter is a hearty winter treat that's rich in texture and aroma, and is lovely served warm with a Pinot Noir. I usually prepare one bruschetta per person as a starter, but it's a great evening snack as well, for when you're all snuggled up with a blanket around the fireplace with a glass of red in hand.

30g / ¼ cup all-purpose flour

¼ teaspoon crushed red pepper flakes

Sea salt and coarsely ground black pepper

4 lamb kidneys

1 tablespoon salted butter

60ml / ¼ cup white wine

4 small slices baguettes, toasted

1 smoked garlic clove, halved (optional; see Tip)

4 tablespoons foie gras

2 tablespoons roughly chopped fresh flat-leaf parsley

In a small bowl, combine the flour and red pepper flakes, and season with salt and pepper to taste.

Butterfly the kidneys, cutting out and discarding the white core. Toss and coat the kidney pieces in the flour mixture.

In a small skillet set over medium heat, melt the butter. Add the white wine and cook until slightly reduced, 1 to 2 minutes. Add the floured kidneys and fry until cooked through, 2 to 3 minutes per side.

Rub the toasted bread slices with the garlic, if desired. Slather each of the slices with 1 tablespoon of foie gras, before topping with 2 kidney halves. Drizzle any remaining juices left in the skillet over the kidneys, and garnish with parsley and a sprinkle of salt. Serve immediately.

TIP: Smoked garlic has a delicious flavor that I love in this dish. You can find it at some specialty groceries or online, though the dish is already full of flavor.

FIG AND PECAN NO-KNEAD BREAD

Makes 1 loaf

I first learned about "no-knead" bread from a friend of mine in Norway, Ina Johnsen, who runs a great Norwegian food blog called *Mat På Bordet*. She had come across this way of making bread on her travels to New York, and even though I love kneading dough just the way my mother does, I really enjoy this recipe. Easy to make, with a lengthier rising period, it's simply baked in a cast-iron casserole in the oven, resulting in a country-style bread with a crunchy crust and a moist and airy interior. Slather slices of it with butter when it's warm out of the oven, or toast it and top with a cinnamon compound butter for a sweet treat with your afternoon tea. It keeps for four or five days.

410g / 3 cups plus ⅓ cup all-purpose flour, plus more for rising and baking

125g / 1 cup whole-wheat flour

Pinch of sea salt

60g / ½ cup pecans, roughly chopped

5 dried figs, stemmed and finely chopped

500ml / 2 cups plus 2 tablespoons lukewarm water

½ teaspoon active dry yeast

1 generous tablespoon honey

In a large bowl, combine both flours together with the salt. In a dry pan set over medium to low heat, toast the pecans for 5 minutes, until golden and slightly crunchy. Add the toasted pecans to the flour mixture along with the figs. Mix well. In a small bowl mix the lukewarm water with the yeast and honey. Make a well in the middle of the flour mixture, and pour in the liquid. Combine well with a wooden spoon until you have a wet dough. Cover the bowl with a kitchen towel, and place in a warm, draft-free location to rise for 12 to 18 hours. You can even leave it for up to 24 hours; you'll get the best results if it rises between 18 to 24 hours, as more flavor may develop.

After the rising period, flour a large sheet of parchment paper on a flat surface and empty the dough out of the bowl. With a flexible spatula fold the dough into itself 4 to 6 times. Cover the dough with the bowl turned upside down, and let it rise again for another 2 hours on the kitchen counter.

Thirty minutes before the dough is ready to be baked, preheat the oven to 250°C / 480°F, and place a Dutch oven, or an ovenproof cast-iron casserole dish with an ovenproof lid, inside the oven. When the dough is ready to be baked, quickly take the hot dish out of the oven, remove the lid, flour the bottom of the dish generously, and dump the dough inside. Don't be discouraged if the dough is quite wet; simply scrape it out of the bowl with a flexible spatula and arrange it in the middle of the dish.

Cover with the lid, turn the heat down to 220°C / 425°F, and bake for 30 minutes. Remove the lid and bake for 15 to 18 minutes more, until the crust is golden. The bread will now have a lovely crunchy crust. Turn the bread out onto a wire rack and let it rest 5 to 7 minutes before serving.

WALDORF SALAD

Serves 4 to 6

On New Year's Eve and other special occasions, my mother makes her fresh and creamy Waldorf salad. Even though it's quite rich, the apples, grapes, lemon juice, and cabbage add just the right amount of acidity to cut through the cream. It never fails to complete our New Year's Eve meal. It's a great side for any meat dish and is particularly good with the Norwegian Pork Belly (page 39). Serve it freshly made, as the cream might separate if it sits for a few hours before serving.

300ml / 1¼ cups double cream / heavy cream	1 Granny Smith apple, cored and cut into bite-size pieces	3 canned or fresh pineapple rings (drained if canned), chopped
150ml / ½ cup plus 2 tablespoons mayonnaise	200g / 7 ounces white cabbage, cored, finely sliced	200g / 7 ounces green seedless grapes, halved lengthwise
1 tablespoon sugar	1 to 2 celery stalks, thinly sliced	100g / 1 cup walnuts, roughly chopped
Juice of ½ lemon		

In a small bowl, beat the cream until soft peaks form. Gently fold in the mayonnaise, sugar, and lemon juice. Add the diced apple to the cream mixture to prevent the fruit from browning.

In a large bowl, combine the cabbage, celery, and pineapple. Add two-thirds of the grapes and walnuts and stir well. Fold in the cream mixture until well combined, and refrigerate for 5 to 10 minutes. Garnish with the remaining grapes and walnuts before serving.

TRUFFLED YORKSHIRE PUDDING WITH ONION GRAVY

Serves 4 to 6

We didn't watch much TV growing up, but one show was a must—a British TV series from the '80s called *The Darling Buds of May*. It was there, during family evenings gathered around the telly for the weekly viewing of the show, that we discovered Yorkshire pudding. The end credits hadn't even begun rolling over the screen before my mother, in true pre-Internet style, picked up the phone to call a trusted English source to get the recipe. As a family we fell in love with the golden, puffed crust, and the way it so perfectly serves as a vehicle to soak up gravy. I brought this recipe with me to my English cottage and made it my own, tweaking it and adding flavors that I love. My version includes truffle oil and a dash of mustard, which lends a decadent aroma to this humble pudding and gives it a bit of body. It's a must for your Sunday roast, and a tasty side to many hearty meat dishes.

---

3 medium eggs

150ml / ½ cup plus 2 tablespoons
    whole milk

70g / ½ cup all-purpose flour

1 tablespoon Dijon mustard

4 tablespoons truffle oil

Pinch of sea salt

Onion Gravy (recipe follows)

Preheat the oven to 200°C / 400°F.

In a medium bowl, whisk together the eggs, milk, flour, mustard, 1 tablespoon of truffle oil, and salt. Let the batter rest, covered, for 15 minutes.

Add the remaining tablespoons of truffle oil to a 20 × 30-centimeter / 8 × 12-inch baking dish. Place in the oven for 10 minutes.

Lower the heat to 180°C / 350°F.

Remove the dish from the oven and quickly pour the batter into the hot dish. Return the dish to the oven and bake, without opening the door, until the pudding is puffed up and golden brown, 20 to 22 minutes. Cut into squares and serve warm with onion gravy.

ONION GRAVY

Serves 4

---

1 tablespoon salted butter

4 medium red onions, halved and thinly sliced

1 carrot, chopped

50g / ¼ cup sugar

100ml / scant ½ cup red wine vinegar

500ml / 2 cups plus 2 tablespoons beef stock

1½ tablespoons all-purpose flour

½ teaspoon sea salt

½ teaspoon coarsely ground black pepper

In a medium saucepan set over medium heat, melt the butter. Add the onions, carrot, and sugar, and cook, stirring constantly, until the sugar is browned, 3 to 4 minutes. Add the vinegar and cook, stirring, until the sugar has dissolved completely, 2 to 3 minutes.

In a glass jar, combine 100ml / a scant ½ cup of the stock with the flour. Place the lid on tightly and shake vigorously until there are no lumps. Pour the flour mixture and the remaining stock into the pan of vegetables, increase the heat to high, and bring to a boil. Reduce the heat to low and cook until thickened, 25 to 30 minutes. Season with salt and pepper.

TIP: Any drippings you may have from cooking meat can be added before seasoning to enhance the flavor and depth of the gravy.

WARM SALMON, MINT, AND POTATO SALAD

Serves 4

In Norway, fresh wild salmon is readily available and is found in abundance. This pink fish is a staple in Scandinavian cooking and is at its best when not farmed. Should you not be able to find salmon at your local fishmonger, you can substitute with freshly caught trout. You can make both the potatoes and salmon in advance and enjoy the salad chilled, or quickly warm it up before adding the dressing, cucumber, dill, green onions, and mint. I love serving it as a starter or for lunch. Either way you choose, be sure to serve it with a dry white wine.

500g / 1 pound new potatoes, scrubbed

1 tablespoon salted butter

500g / 1 pound salmon fillets

150ml / ½ cup plus 1 tablespoon Greek or plain yogurt

¼ teaspoon crushed red pepper flakes

1 heaping tablespoon roughly chopped fresh dill, plus more for garnish

½ teaspoon sea salt

3 tablespoons diced English cucumber

1 Granny Smith apple, peeled, cored, and chopped

Juice of ¼ lemon

Coarsely ground black pepper

1 heaping tablespoon roughly chopped fresh mint

15g / 2 tablespoons green onions / scallions, trimmed and sliced, for garnish

---

Put the potatoes in a medium saucepan set over medium heat, cover with water, and bring to a boil. Cook until tender, 18 to 20 minutes. Drain and set aside. When cool enough to handle, cut each potato in half.

In a medium skillet set over medium heat, melt the butter. Add the salmon and cook until cooked through, 4 to 5 minutes per side. Transfer the salmon to a cutting board and remove the skin if present, before shredding the flesh with a fork.

In a medium bowl, combine the yogurt, red pepper flakes, dill, salt, cucumber, apple, and lemon juice. Season generously with black pepper and mint.

Arrange the potatoes in serving bowls, evenly distribute the shredded salmon among them, then place a dollop of the yogurt mixture on top. Garnish with the mint, scallions, and additional dill, and serve.

NO-KNEAD COUNTRY LOAF

Makes 1 loaf

Little beats waking up to the aromas of bread baking in the oven. To me, it's these comforting smells that make a house a home. I usually make this bread a couple of times a week. With a golden crust and a moist inside, it's my go-to recipe. I like to mix up the dough midafternoon and let it sit overnight. The next day, I'll get up early to bake it before the house awakens. When friends and family come to visit, I love the gesture of serving a freshly baked loaf for breakfast, as few things are more welcoming than baked goods. Serve it warm, with butter and honey, or garnish as you would your favorite bread.

535g / 3⅔ cups all-purpose flour, plus additional for rising and baking

Pinch of sea salt

500ml / 2 cups plus 2 tablespoons lukewarm water

½ teaspoon active dry yeast

1 generous tablespoon honey

In a large bowl, combine the flour and the salt. In a small bowl, mix the lukewarm water with the yeast and honey. Make a well in the middle of the flour and pour in the liquid, mixing well with a wooden spoon until a wet dough forms. Cover the bowl with a kitchen towel and place in a warm, draft-free location to rise for 12 to 18 hours.

After the rising period, use a flexible spatula to fold the dough into itself 4 to 6 times. Cover the dough again, and let it rise for another 2 hours on the kitchen counter.

Thirty minutes before baking, preheat the oven to 250°C / 480°F, and place a Dutch oven, or an ovenproof cast-iron casserole dish with the lid on, inside the oven. When the dough is ready to be baked, quickly take the dish out of the oven, remove the lid, flour the bottom of the dish generously, and dump the dough inside. Don't be discouraged if the dough is quite wet; simply scrape it off with a flexible spatula and arrange it in the middle of the dish. Cover, turn the heat down to 220°C / 425°F, and bake for 30 minutes. After 30 minutes, remove the lid and bake for another 15 minutes. The bread will now have a lovely golden crust. Let it rest 5 to 7 minutes on a wire rack before serving.

TARRAGON BUTTER BAKED SCALLOPS

Serves 6

This is a darling little recipe for a quick and easy starter. Prepare all the ingredients in advance, simply arrange them in the scallop shells and pop them in the oven right before your guests take their seats at the table. Serve the scallops warm out of the oven in their shells, with a glass of sparkling wine and a basket of torn sourdough bread or No-Knead Country Loaf (page 32) to dip in and mop up the tarragon sauce. If you can't purchase fresh scallops, you can use frozen and purchase the shells separately. If the scallops are small, place two to three in each shell. Rinse and keep the shell to use again.

3½ tablespoons salted butter, room temperature

Juice of ¼ lemon

1 shallot, finely chopped

1 tablespoon finely chopped fresh tarragon

¼ teaspoon crushed red pepper flakes

Sea salt and coarsely ground black pepper

6 scallops, in their shells

Torn sourdough bread, for serving

Preheat the oven to 220°C / 425°F.

In a mortar and pestle, pound the butter, lemon juice, shallot, tarragon, red pepper flakes, salt, and black pepper until well combined.

Arrange the scallops, in their shells, on a large baking sheet. Divide the tarragon butter evenly among the scallops.

Bake until just cooked through, 5 to 7 minutes. Serve hot, with bread on the side to soak up the juices from the shell.

CHORIZO MACARONI AND CHEESE

Serves 4 to 6

When I was thirteen I visited my sister, who was living in America at the time. I fell in love with macaroni and cheese—the unsophisticated version that comes in a blue box with powdered cheese in a sash. I thought it was the most delicious treat, and filled up my suitcase with these boxes upon my return to Norway. My love for the dish remains, though thankfully my taste buds have outgrown the contents of the blue boxes. These days, I make it with my favorite cheeses and spicy chorizo for a bit more zing. Spicy or not, be sure to choose a quality chorizo. Serve this dish warm with a sprinkle of coarsely ground black pepper and a chilled crisp Riesling.

1½L / 6⅓ cups water

1 chicken stock cube / bouillon

350g / 12 ounces spiral pasta

2 tablespoons all-purpose flour

2 teaspoons Dijon mustard

400ml / 1⅔ cups whole milk

3 tablespoons salted butter

1 to 2 garlic cloves, finely chopped

100g / 3½ ounces chorizo, finely chopped

100ml / ⅓ cup plus 1 tablespoon double cream / heavy cream

100g / 3½ ounces mature cheddar, grated

100g / 3½ ounces Taleggio, chopped

100g / 3½ ounces Gruyère, grated

Sea salt and coarsely ground black pepper

2 tablespoons grated Parmesan

In a medium saucepan set over medium heat, stir together the water and the chicken bouillon until the cube is dissolved. Bring the mixture to a boil. Add the pasta and cook according to the package instructions until al dente. (You may not need to salt the pasta water since the bouillon can be quite salty.) Reserve 90ml / ⅓ cup of the pasta water, then drain the pasta.

In a jar, combine the flour, mustard, and 150ml / ½ cup of milk, screw on the lid, and shake until the mixture is free of lumps.

Preheat the oven to 180°C / 350°F. In a large saucepan set over medium heat, combine the butter, garlic, and chorizo and cook, stirring, for 1 minute. Add the mustard mixture to the pan and cook, stirring, for 1 to 2 minutes. Gradually whisk in the cream, reserved pasta cooking water, and remaining milk, until the sauce is smooth and lump-free. Simmer, whisking constantly, until thickened slightly, 2 to 3 minutes. Remove the pan from the heat and add the cheddar, Taleggio, and Gruyère. Tip the pasta into the sauce and stir until combined. Season with salt and pepper to taste. Pour the mixture into a medium baking dish and sprinkle with the Parmesan.

Bake until lightly golden on top, 18 to 20 minutes.

NORWEGIAN PORK BELLY
WITH MUSTARD COLESLAW
AND BROWN GRAVY

RIBBE

Serves 6 to 8

Because my mother yearned to start her very own Christmas traditions, and perhaps to make a feisty statement when she married my father, she chose to politely turn down her mother-in-law's suggestion to carry on with the family tradition of making *pinnekjøtt*, a smoked lamb dish, on December 24. She instead began making *ribbe*, a thick pork belly with the crunchiest crackling, and it has been a staple piece on our Christmas Eve table ever since. And my father has never complained, at least as far as I know. My family only serves this dish at Christmas, with warm red cabbage stew and boiled potatoes, but I enjoy making it throughout winter. Paired with my Truffled Yorkshire Pudding (page 28), mustard coleslaw, and brown gravy, it's a celebratory feast. Make sure you get your butcher to give you the Norwegian cut of pork belly. This cut is thicker than other pork belly cuts, where both skin (for crackling) and bones are present.

2kg / 4½ pounds pork belly, 5 to 8 centimeters / 2 to 3 inches thick, on the bone, with skin on	Sea salt and coarsely ground black pepper 200ml / ¾ cup plus 1 tablespoon water	Mustard Coleslaw (recipe follows) Brown Gravy (recipe follows)

Using a very sharp knife, slice the skin of the pork belly to score it both horizontally and vertically almost down to the bones. Season the pork generously with salt and pepper, cover it with foil, and refrigerate it for 2 to 3 days.

When you're ready to cook the pork, remove it from the fridge, uncover it, and bring it to room temperature, about 45 minutes.

Preheat the oven to 220°C / 425°F.

recipe continues

Pour the water into a large baking dish with 2-centimeter / ¾-inch-high sides. Place a small, ovenproof plate upside down in the middle of the dish and center the pork belly, scored side facing up, on the plate so the crackling will bake better. The plate will create a gentle curve to the meat, opening up the cracks in the skin to allow the fat to drip and the skin to crisp up. Cover the whole baking dish tightly with foil.

Bake for 45 minutes. Remove the foil and reduce the oven temperature to 180°C / 350°F. Bake for another 1 to 1½ hours for a pork belly that is 5 to 7 centimeters / about 2 inches thick, or 2 to 2½ hours for pork belly (Norwegian style) that is 7 to 8 centimeters / about 3 inches thick. Keep an eye on the meat and drippings, adding a bit of water to the baking dish to keep it from drying out and burning the drippings. Turn the oven off, and let it cool in the oven with the door slightly ajar for 15 to 20 minutes.

Transfer the pork to a cutting board and cut it into thick slices before serving warm, or cold.

TIP: With any leftover meat, arrange in a sandwich the next day with some mustard or left over coleslaw.

MUSTARD COLESLAW

Serves 4 to 6

3 tablespoons sour cream	3 teaspoons Colman's mustard powder	100g / 3½ ounces purple cabbage, finely sliced
3 tablespoons mayonnaise	2 tablespoons sugar	2 small Granny Smith apples, peeled, cored, and grated
4 tablespoons fresh lemon juice	200g / 7 ounces white cabbage, finely sliced	1 carrot, grated

In a large bowl, combine the sour cream, mayonnaise, lemon juice, mustard powder, and sugar. Add the cabbage, apples, and carrot to the dressing and gently fold together until combined and mixed through.

BROWN GRAVY

Serves 4 to 6

The Norwegian brown goat's cheese adds a lovely depth and sweetness to this gravy that takes it to the next level, but it's an optional addition and not at all necessary.

400ml / 1²/₃ cups beef stock

200ml / ³/₄ cup plus 1 tablespoon whole milk

3 tablespoons salted butter

3 tablespoons all-purpose flour

Pan drippings from Marie's Meatballs (page 113) or Norwegian Pork Belly (page 39) (optional)

1 tablespoon Norwegian brown goat's cheese, grated (optional)

¼ teaspoon sea salt

½ teaspoon coarsely ground black pepper

In a medium saucepan set over medium-low heat, combine the stock with the milk and warm for 5 to 7 minutes. Pour into a bowl and set aside.

In the same saucepan set over medium heat, melt the butter. While stirring constantly, add the flour and cook, stirring, until browned, 4 to 5 minutes. Reduce the heat to medium-low, and pour in the milk mixture in a thin stream, stirring vigorously to avoid lumps. Cook, stirring constantly, until you have a thick sauce, 5 to 8 minutes. If you have any drippings from making the meatballs or pork belly, stir them in at this point, along with the goat cheese, if using. Season with salt and pepper. Simmer over low heat and cook until thickened, 4 to 5 minutes. Serve warm.

NORWEGIAN SWEET RICE CREAM PORRIDGE WITH CINNAMON

RISENGRYNSGRØT

Serves 4 to 6

Every Christmas Eve my mother serves this sweet rice-and-milk porridge for lunch, which is a tradition in Norway. She'll hide one blanched almond in it for a lucky family member to find. If swallowed, no prize will be given, but if you can show it whole on your spoon, you'll win a marzipan pig for dessert. We all get quite competitive, searching our bowls with great eagerness, and consuming way more than we should. To many non-Norwegians, it may be unfamiliar to have a sweet main course, but in Norway, this is served not only for Christmas but for dinner throughout the year, and is one of my favorite porridges.

400ml / 1²/₃ cups water

350g / 1²/₃ cups short-grain rice or risotto rice or Scandinavian *grøtris*

1.35L / 5³/₄ cups whole milk

1 teaspoon sea salt

Ground cinnamon, for serving

Sugar, for serving

Salted butter, for serving

In a large saucepan set over medium heat, bring the water to a boil. Add the rice, reduce the heat to low, cover, and simmer until the water is absorbed completely, 15 to 20 minutes, occasionally giving it a gentle stir to prevent any sticking. Add the milk and bring to a boil, then reduce the heat to low. Let cook, covered, stirring occasionally, until the porridge has a creamy consistency, 45 to 50 minutes. Feel free to add more milk if you like. Season with salt.

Serve hot in individual bowls with a sprinkle of cinnamon and sugar and a knob of salted butter in the middle.

TIP: When the porridge has been brought to a boil, my mother takes it off the stove, wraps it in a towel and then a duvet or blanket, and leaves it to sit for 1 to 2 hours, adding milk if the porridge is too thick. This makes it ideal to put in the back of the car, while on a road trip, or on your way to visit a friend. I have many fond memories of her unveiling it from the trunk of the car for an autumn picnic, or bringing supper to friends.

TRUFFLED VEGETABLE
TOAD-IN-THE-HOLE

Serves 4

I'm partial to a good toad-in-the-hole, which is a dish I was introduced to after moving to England. The mixture of spiced sausages, like Cumberland sausage, all nestled in Yorkshire pudding, is a quick supper typically made on cold and dark days of the year, but I wanted to see if I could make it with vegetables and still keep it full of flavor. This vegetarian option is a delightful version of the more traditional one and is best eaten immediately. When you bake it, make sure not to open the oven door to have a peek, as the pudding will deflate. I usually serve it with a chilled cloudy dry cider, such as Old Rosie. For a more prominent truffle flavor, finely slice a quarter of a small black truffle and add it to the batter.

3 medium eggs

150ml / ½ cup plus 2 tablespoons whole milk

70g / ½ cup all-purpose flour

2 tablespoons whole-grain Dijon mustard

4 tablespoons truffle oil

Sea salt

200g / 7 ounces Chantenay carrots

150g / 5 ounces green beans, snapped in half

2 tablespoons unsalted butter

1 medium yellow onion, cut into 1-centimeter / ⅓-inch-thick wedges

2 garlic cloves, sliced

150g / 1 cup cherry tomatoes, halved

1 tablespoon finely chopped fresh basil

½ teaspoon finely chopped fresh thyme

½ teaspoon finely chopped fresh rosemary

Coarsely ground black pepper

Onion Gravy (page 29), for serving

Preheat the oven to 200°C / 400°F.

In a medium bowl, beat together the eggs, milk, flour, 1 tablespoon of mustard, 1 tablespoon of truffle oil, and a generous pinch of salt. Let the batter stand for 15 minutes.

Fill a large saucepan with 5 centimeters / 2 inches of water, place a steamer basket on top, and set the pan over high heat. When the water begins to boil put the carrots and green beans into the steamer basket, cover the pan, and

recipe continues

steam until just tender, 4 to 5 minutes. Remove from the heat and set aside.

Add the remaining tablespoons of truffle oil to a 20 × 30-centimeter / 8 × 13-inch baking dish. Place the dish in the oven for 10 minutes to heat it.

In a large skillet set over medium heat, melt the butter. Add the onion, garlic, and a generous pinch of salt. Cook, stirring, until soft, 3 to 5 minutes. Add the green beans to the skillet and cook, stirring, 3 to 4 minutes. Add the carrots, tomatoes, basil, thyme, rosemary, and the remaining tablespoon of mustard and stir well. Season to taste with salt and pepper.

Reduce the oven temperature to 180°C / 350°F.

Remove the baking dish from the oven and immediately pour in the batter. Scatter the vegetables on top.

Bake until the pudding is fluffy and golden, 18 to 20 minutes. Do not open the oven door while baking, as the pudding will deflate. Serve hot, straight out of oven with the onion gravy on the side.

CREAMY FISH SOUP WITH CLAMS

Serves 4

I grew up on a fjord island with fresh seafood right on my doorstep. My father would occasionally take me fishing in our small boat, and we'd catch cod and mackerel, depending on the time of the year. We were also lucky to have a local fisherman named Elias, who came to our home weekly with his catch in a bag on the back of his blue moped, and every now and then he'd bring us salmon. This creamy soup is full of flavor and texture and is delicious served with a chilled dry white wine. I find that it's just as good during the colder months of the year as it is during spring and summer.

3 tablespoons unsalted butter

1 fennel bulb, roughly chopped

1 yellow onion, roughly chopped

1 celery stalk, roughly chopped

1 leek, cleaned well and finely chopped

3 garlic cloves, finely chopped

2 tablespoons finely chopped fresh flat-leaf parsley

2 tablespoons finely chopped fresh thyme

2 tablespoons finely chopped fresh basil

200ml / ¾ cup plus 1 tablespoon dry white wine

200g / 7 ounces clams, in their shells

2 tablespoons water

500ml / 2 cups plus 2 tablespoons fish stock

400g / 14 ounces salmon fillets, cut into cubes

100ml / scant ½ cup double cream / heavy cream

Sea salt and coarsely ground black pepper

Set a large saucepan over medium heat, and melt the butter. Add the fennel, onion, celery, leek, garlic, parsley, thyme, and basil and cook, stirring occasionally, until the vegetables are soft, 5 to 6 minutes. Add the wine and let the vegetables steep for 5 to 6 minutes.

In a separate medium saucepan set over medium heat, combine the clams and water. Cover, bring to a simmer, and cook until the shells open, 5 to 10 minutes. Drain the clams, discarding any clams that did not open.

Add the stock to the vegetable mixture and let it simmer for 2 to 3 minutes. Add the salmon fillets to the soup and simmer for 2 to 3 more minutes. Stir in the cream, and season with salt and pepper to taste before adding the clams. Simmer for another 1 to 2 minutes. Serve hot.

WARMING LAMB AND CABBAGE STEW

FÅRIKÅL

Serves 4 to 6

We have a whole day in Norway that is dedicated to this humble, yet ever-so-tasty cabbage and lamb stew. The last Thursday in September every year is *Fårikålens dag,* "the Day of Fårikål," and many Norwegians will serve up this dish true to tradition, inviting friends and family over to celebrate. My mother makes this often during winter, and it was one of the first dishes I made when I moved to my English cottage. Dead simple to make, you'll be surprised at how much flavor there is in this stew. The meat has to be cooked on the bone so the marrow infuses and nourishes the soup. It's just as good, if not better, the next day, as the flavors will have had time to develop further.

---

1 (1½kg / 3.3-pound) head white cabbage

1½kg / 3.3 pounds lamb on the bone (shoulder, shank, or neck), cut into small pieces

Sea salt

3 teaspoons whole black peppercorns

350ml / 1½ cups water, plus more for the potatoes

10 to 12 whole King Edward potatoes, peeled

Remove the outer leaves of the cabbage, then cut the cabbage into quarters through the core. Cut each quarter into 3 to 4 wedges, making sure to keep part of the core on each wedge, as this will hold the cabbage together.

In a large pot, place a layer of meat, followed by a layer of cabbage. Season with salt and peppercorns. Repeat the layers until all of the meat and cabbage have been used. (Traditionally the last layer should be cabbage.) Pour enough water over the meat and cabbage to cover it, cover the pan, and bring to a boil over medium-high heat. Reduce the heat to low and simmer for 2½ to 3 hours, checking the water level occasionally to make sure the dish doesn't dry out. It is ready when the lamb is tender and falling off the bone.

About 30 minutes before the stew is ready, bring a large pot of water to a boil over high heat. Add the potatoes, reduce the heat to low, and gently simmer until soft, 20 to 25 minutes.

To serve, place the potatoes in individual bowls, and ladle stew on top.

BUTTER BAKED COD WITH SAFFRON AND PARSLEY SAUCE

Serves 4

My mother would eye up our local fisherman Elias's fish, make her selection, and immediately bring it inside to gut and rinse before freezing or preparing. I remember how exciting it was to help her prepare fresh cod, sometimes frying it in butter, other times tossing it in seasoned flour before frying it crisp in a pan, or perhaps boiling it whole. My mother rarely steamed or baked the fish, though those are indeed my preferred methods today. In this recipe, creating little parcels in which to bake the cod locks in the flavor. Serve warm with your favorite chilled white wine.

1 tablespoon plus 4 teaspoons salted butter

4 dry bay leaves

4 (250g / 8½-ounce) cod fillets

Sea salt and coarsely ground black pepper

1 tablespoon all-purpose flour

225ml / scant 1 cup vegetable stock

½ teaspoon high-quality ground saffron

½ tablespoon sour cream

½ tablespoon roughly chopped fresh flat-leaf parsley, plus more for garnish

1 tablespoon capers, for garnish

Preheat the oven to 200°C / 400°F.

Cut 4 pieces of parchment paper to 23 × 36-centimeter / 9 × 14-inch rectangles and soak them in water. Squeeze the water out. Place 1 teaspoon of butter and a bay leaf in the middle of each piece of parchment, then place a cod fillet on top, seasoning it generously with salt and pepper. Wrap the parchment around the cod, completely covering the fish, and tie it tightly with a piece of kitchen twine to ensure that the parcels stay closed during baking. Place the parcels on a large baking sheet.

Bake on the middle rack until cooked through, 15 to 18 minutes.

Meanwhile, make the sauce. In a small saucepan set over medium-low heat, melt 1 tablespoon of the butter. Add the flour and stir constantly for 1 to 2 minutes. While continuing to stir, pour the stock into the pan in a thin stream. Increase the heat to medium and bring the sauce to a boil. Cook until it is smooth and lump-free, for 3 to 4 minutes (strain the sauce, if needed).

Reduce the heat to low, add the saffron, and let it infuse in the sauce while stirring, 2 to 3 minutes. Stir in the sour cream and heat through, 1 to 2 minutes. Season to taste with salt and pepper, and add the parsley.

Remove the fish from the oven and place one parcel on each plate. Cut open the parcels at the table. Serve the cod warm with a generous amount of sauce, and garnish with the capers.

MY FATHER'S TROLL CREAM

Serves 4 to 6

Most nights when I was a little girl, I'd beg my father to tell me the story of the boy with the dog that had eagle wings. He'd turn off the light, get into character, and say "Spread your eagle wings!" as he stretched out his arms as far as they'd reach. Night after night, he'd make up another chapter of his fairy tale, in which the pair would fly deep into the mountain kingdom of Jotunheimen to visit the trolls. After each big meal that the trolls enjoyed, they would empty their baskets of freshly picked ruby-red cranberries and make a dessert called "Troll Cream," a pink, fluffy, tart-and-sweet treat that happened to be my father's favorite. Every year on my father's birthday, which is the day before Christmas Eve, my mother would serve this delicious dessert, and I'd glance over at my father as he tucked into it, one heaping spoonful after another, to see if, by some magic, the trolls from his bedtime stories would join us. They haven't yet, but perhaps one day they will. This cream, incredibly easy to make and quick to put together right before your guests arrive, will stay fluffy and firm for a few hours if kept in the fridge, but it is best served immediately.

500g / 4 cups fresh cranberries	240g / 1¼ cups sugar	1 egg white

In a large bowl, combine all the ingredients. Using an electric hand mixer on medium speed, beat everything together until a pink foam with peaks forms, 7 to 10 minutes. Serve immediately.

recipe continues

FROZEN TROLL CREAM

Serves 4 to 6

Native to the northern hemisphere, and with a short season, fresh cranberries aren't readily available for everyone. So I've included a recipe using frozen cranberries. The end results are nearly the same as the original, though there's a freshness and overall lightness when the berries are in season.

2 egg whites	480g / 2¼ cups plus 2 tablespoons sugar	300g / 2⅓ cups frozen cranberries, half of them thawed

In a large bowl, using an electric hand mixer on medium speed, beat the egg whites until soft peaks form, 5 to 6 minutes. With the mixer still running, gradually add the sugar little by little until incorporated, 5 to 8 minutes.

In a small bowl, mash the thawed berries with a fork.

Fold the mashed berries into the meringue and whisk until combined and the meringue is pink. Fold the frozen cranberries into the mixture and serve immediately.

SAFFRON AND VANILLA
POACHED PEARS

Serves 6

Every time my mother opened the spice cupboard in our kitchen, I would be instantly transported to far-flung places. Star anise, cardamom, cinnamon, saffron, rosewater, almond essence, and vanilla—I thought it so exciting when she cooked or baked with these aromatic ingredients. Saffron and vanilla in particular carry with them a sense of the exotic, and I use them in my kitchen here in the countryside more often than not. Whenever I head down to the local butcher in Tisbury, where I live now, to stock up on saffron, they ask, "Again?" in bewilderment, wondering where the last batch went. It's the secret ingredient in many of my baked goods, as well as savory supper dishes such as my Risotto Milanese (page 108), and of course in desserts. Not only does saffron lend its distinctive yellow color to anything it's used in, but its distinctive aroma is unmistakable. Here, the pears take on a golden glow when poached in the saffron and Vin Santo mixture, which makes them really stand out next to a dollop of whipped cream or vanilla ice cream. Though this can be eaten chilled, I prefer serving the pears warm. You can make the poached pears up to two days in advance and store them in the fridge in an airtight container. Serve with a side of My Mother's Whipped Cream (page 125) and drizzle the rest of the Vin Santo-and-pear syrup over top.

---

6 firm pears, such as Packham or Forelle (or any relatively firm variety)

1 vanilla bean

1½ teaspoons saffron

80g / 6 tablespoons caster sugar / superfine sugar

700ml / 3 cups Vin Santo or your favorite white grape-based dessert wine

½ batch My Mother's Whipped Cream (page 125), for serving

Peel each pear, leaving the stems on, and cut all the pears at the bases to create a stable bottom.

Split the vanilla bean lengthwise and use the back of a knife to scrape out the seeds. Put the seeds in a medium saucepan with high sides set over medium

recipe continues

heat, toss in the pod, then add the saffron, sugar, and wine. Bring the mixture to a boil. Arrange the pears in the saucepan so that they stand upright. Bring the mixture back to a boil, then reduce the heat to low and cover the pan. Simmer, turning the pears every 5 minutes to ensure they are well coated with the liquid and cooked evenly on all sides, until cooked through, 25 to 30 minutes. Test with a skewer; the pears should be tender throughout, but still retain their shape. Transfer the pears to a plate. Simmer the wine mixture over medium heat until it has reduced by half to a syrup consistency, 10 to 12 minutes.

Return the pears to the syrup and keep warm until ready to serve. To serve, slice each pear in half lengthwise, then place both halves on a dessert plate with a dollop of whipped cream and a drizzle of the reserved syrup. Serve immediately.

OLGA'S CARAMEL PUDDING

Serves 6 to 8

After church on Sundays, my family would pile into the car and make our way out of the city, across the river and to my grandparents' little oasis on the outskirts of the neighboring town called Sarpsborg. Dressed in an apron over her Sunday best, my grandmother would greet us with warm hugs and a table set with crystal glasses and silverware. Only the finest would do on a Sunday. Being a woman who was always prepared, dinner would be kept in the warming cupboard, water would be chilling in a pretty glass jug in the fridge, and on the shelf below we'd find her homemade dessert, a repertoire that rotated between chocolate pudding and caramel pudding. My brother and I would eagerly run up the stairs to the kitchen to discover which one would be served after dinner. As a child, her chocolate pudding was my very favorite, yet as I grew older, I began to crave her caramel pudding. Drizzled with dark caramel sauce, each silky-smooth spoonful oozes with old-school decadence in the most glorious way. Serve it at room temperature with warmed caramel sauce, paired with a golden dessert wine like Vin Santo or a cup of black coffee. Be sure to make more than needed, as one helping is simply never enough. This pudding is self-saucing.

4 tablespoons caster sugar / superfine sugar	150ml / ½ cup plus 3 tablespoons double cream / heavy cream	Caramel Sauce (recipe follows), for serving
3 medium eggs	170g / ¾ cup caster sugar / superfine sugar	½ batch My Mother's Whipped Cream (page 125), for serving
300ml / 1¼ cups whole milk	½ teaspoon vanilla paste	

Preheat the oven to 150°C / 300°F with a rack placed in the middle.

In a medium skillet set over low heat, melt the 2 tablespoons of sugar and let it cook, occasionally swirling the pan but not stirring, until it becomes golden in color, 3 to 4 minutes. Pour the golden sugar into a 9 × 24-centimeter / 3½ × 9½-inch baking dish and set aside. It will harden and become almost like toffee; don't be concerned, it will soften when baked.

recipe continues

In a medium bowl, beat the eggs lightly. Add the milk, cream, 170g / ¾ cup of sugar, and vanilla paste and whisk until well combined. Pour the mixture into the baking dish, over the set sugar. Place that dish into a large, deep roasting pan and pour piping hot water (but not boiling, as this will create bubbles inside the caramel pudding) into the larger pan until it reaches halfway up the sides of the baking dish.

Place the roasting pan on the middle oven rack and bake until the pudding is golden and a wooden skewer inserted in the center comes out clean, 55 to 60 minutes. Monitor the water, lowering the oven temperature if necessary, while the pudding cooks to ensure that it does not boil. Turn the oven off, and leave the pudding to cool in the oven with the door slightly ajar for about 15 minutes.

Once completely cool, refrigerate the pudding overnight, or serve as is.

Remove the pudding from the refrigerator 30 minutes before serving so that it can come to room temperature, if you've refrigerated it overnight. Loosen the sides by running a knife around the edges of the dish. Place a serving platter over the pudding, and turn it upside down to dislodge the pudding from the baking dish. Cut the pudding into slices and serve each slice with a scoop of the caramel sauce from the baking dish and a dollop of whipped cream.

TIP: To allow all the flavors to blend together and develop, don't skip the overnight stay in the refrigerator. Just be sure to let the pudding warm to room temperature before serving.

NORWEGIAN WAFFLES WITH STRAWBERRIES AND SOUR CREAM

Makes 14 whole waffle plates

In Norway, waffles are possibly the most eaten and appreciated sweet treat. They are just as often eaten cold with cheese as they are enjoyed warm with jam and a dollop of sour cream—everyone has their favorite topping. I think they are best eaten freshly made and served warm with strawberry jam and sour cream, but they will keep for a couple of days wrapped in a kitchen towel, which makes them great for picnics. Coming home from school on a cold day growing up, I would leap with joy when I smelled the warm vanilla-tinged perfume that greeted me as I opened the front door. You can find Norwegian waffle irons in specialty food stores or online.

350g / 2½ cups self-rising flour

200g / 1 cup white caster sugar/ superfine sugar

2 teaspoons baking powder

2 teaspoons ground cardamom

Pinch of sea salt

4 medium eggs

1 teaspoon vanilla paste

600ml / 3 cups whole milk

100g / 6 tablespoons butter, melted, plus more for brushing

Rosewater and Strawberry Jam (Page 187), or any of your favorite jams, for serving

Sour cream, for serving

In a large bowl, combine the flour, sugar, baking powder, cardamom, and salt.

In a medium bowl, combine the eggs, vanilla paste, milk, and melted butter. Add the wet mixture to the dry little by little as you stir, to avoid lumps. Let the batter rest, covered, on the counter for 30 minutes.

Heat the waffle iron and brush both sides with some of the extra melted butter. Add 1 ladleful of the waffle mixture. Cook the waffles until golden, 3 to 4 minutes. Transfer them to a wire rack to cool. Repeat with the remaining batter. Serve warm with strawberry jam, sour cream, and a cup of tea or coffee.

CREMA CATALANA

Serves 6

In a wonky little restaurant in the heart of the Old Town in Nice, I cracked the caramelized sugar on the top of my very first crème brûlée, and there was no going back. The creamy, subtle flavors that slowly melted in my mouth with each spoonful gave me goose bumps of joy.

I worked as a flight attendant for Scandinavian Airlines in my early twenties, and I'd dine out often with the crew during layovers. In Nice, London, Rome, Tel Aviv, and Barcelona, I took full advantage of the different food opportunities each city offered. One evening in Barcelona, after a long day at work, I craved a crème brûlée like the one I had enjoyed in Nice. At a restaurant that night, our waiter suggested I order *crema Catalana*, certain I would love it. This creamy Spanish dessert hits all the familiar notes of a crème brûlée, yet transports you to a citrus garden on a late summer's evening. I love the two desserts equally, which perhaps share the same family tree. This is the version I make now that closely resembles the one I enjoyed in Barcelona that night, and I'm certain you'll come to love it as much as I do. Serve it with a sweet dessert wine like Vin Santo or Marsala.

1 vanilla bean	2 cinnamon sticks	2½ teaspoons cornstarch
1 medium unwaxed orange	4 egg yolks	
500ml / 2 cups plus 2 tablespoons whole milk	115g plus 50g / ¾ cup caster sugar / superfine sugar	

Cut the vanilla bean lengthwise and use the back of a knife to scrape the seeds into a small saucepan, and add the vanilla pod.

Using a vegetable peeler, peel the orange rind into thin ribbons. Place the peel into the saucepan with the vanilla seeds and add the milk and cinnamon sticks. Set the pan over medium-low heat, bring to a simmer, and cook for 5 to 6 minutes. Reduce the heat to low.

Meanwhile, in a medium bowl, beat together the egg yolks, 115g / ½ cup of sugar, and the cornstarch. Slowly pour the egg mixture into the warm milk mixture in a thin stream, whisking constantly. Be careful not to scramble the eggs. You may want to lift the saucepan from the heat while adding the eggs if you're worried about scrambling them. Cook, stirring constantly, until thick, 7 to 10 minutes. Pour the mixture through a fine-mesh sieve into small ramekins or teacups (about 6, depending on size), and sprinkle the remaining sugar over the tops. Let cool until ready to serve.

Just before serving, create the distinct caramelized lid by placing them under the broiler for a minute or two, or use a kitchen torch to brown the layer of sugar.

LEMON CURD

Makes 500ml / 2 cups

Silky smooth and so fresh tasting, this zingy spread was introduced to me after I moved to my English cottage. I make a batch every month, and it's usually gone before I know it. When friends visit, we polish off a jar in a day, so be sure to make a few big batches in one go, perhaps doubling the recipe. I also like to use this as a filling for cakes and in profiteroles. The bright lemony flavor is ever so delightful in comparison to sweet jam. Serve on buttered toast, on Prosecco Scones (page 280) with Clotted Cream (page 124), or with the Lemon Curd Sponge Cake with Pistachios (page 258).

Finely grated zest of 3 unwaxed lemons	125g / 7 tablespoons unsalted butter	200ml / ¾ cup plus 1 tablespoon pourable honey
Juice of 3 to 4 lemons (to taste)		4 large eggs, beaten

Combine the lemon zest and juice, butter, and honey in a medium heatproof bowl, and set the bowl in a medium saucepan of simmering water, with the water reaching halfway up the bowl. Slowly whisk the mixture until the butter is melted and the mixture is silky smooth, 5 to 7 minutes. Remove the bowl from the saucepan, but keep the water simmering.

Test the temperature of the lemon and honey mixture by dabbing some on the back of your hand; it should be lukewarm. Whisking constantly, slowly pour the eggs into the lemon mixture. Place the bowl back over the simmering water and cook, stirring, until the mixture thickens, 15 to 20 minutes. Push the curd through a fine-mesh sieve into a large bowl.

Pour the strained curd into a clean sterilized jar (see Tip), and let cool. The lemon curd will keep in an airtight container in the refrigerator for 1 to 2 weeks.

TIP: There are a few different methods for sterilizing jars. If you have a preferred method, feel free to use that. If not, I usually boil the jars for 10 minutes, and the lids for 5 minutes, before pouring in the contents and screwing the lids on tight.

LIMONCELLO

Makes 2.2L / 9¼ cups

I once spent a summer in Rome studying Baroque art through the University
of Oslo. Our daily lectures were held in churches, museums, and galleries all
over the city. On the weekends I yearned for the beach and would often hop in
the car with a friend and drive down to the Amalfi coast. We usually stayed
in a whitewashed villa that had a citrus garden surrounding its blue pool. In
the evening we'd wander through the garden, inhaling the citrus perfume that
lingered in the warm evening air before taking a seat underneath the trees lit
up by a starry sky and fairy lights to enjoy a nightcap of homemade limoncello.
One October day a few months after I'd moved to England, a friend brought
me a heaping basket of ripe lemons from a nearby estate, and I leapt at the
opportunity of re-creating my Amalfi coast memories in the form of limoncello. Make it when the lemons in your area are at their best, as the quality of
the ingredients is key for so simple a drink.

6 to 7 large unwaxed Sorrento lemons	1L / 4¼ cups vodka (I prefer Black Cow Pure Milk Vodka)	1L / 4¼ cups water 700g / 3½ cups sugar

Zest the lemons with a vegetable peeler into a large bowl or container, making
sure not to include the white pith. Add the vodka and leave, covered, to steep
for 7 days.

On the seventh day, in a medium saucepan set over medium heat, combine
the water and sugar and bring to a low simmer. Cook, stirring, until the sugar
is dissolved, 3 to 5 minutes. Combine the lemon peel and vodka mixture with
the sugar water.

Sterilize (see Tip, page 69) some tall glass bottles large enough to hold the
limoncello.

Strain the liquid and pour it into the bottles. Seal the bottles and refrigerate until cool. The limoncello will keep in a sealed bottle in the refrigerator for
up to 2 months. Serve chilled.

CAMPARI CITRUS MARMALADE

Makes 2L / 2 quarts

Marmalade is such a traditional English spread. I was never a fan of the sharp orange flavor when I was young, but now I love it! Best made with the aromatic Seville oranges that have a relatively short season (from January to February), you can, of course, make it with any high-quality unwaxed organic oranges. I love experimenting with different combinations for my homemade marmalade and have included one of my variations here. It's a bit sweeter than a traditional one and makes a lovely spread for your breakfast toast.

2 unwaxed Seville oranges	Juice of 2 lemons	1½kg / 7½ cups sugar
2 unwaxed grapefruit	1½L / 6⅓ cups water	60ml / ¼ cup Campari

Peel the oranges and grapefruit. Cut out and discard the white membrane, and set aside the peels. Juice the flesh through a strainer, making sure to squeeze out every single drop of juice before discarding the pulp. Finely slice half of the reserved peel from the oranges and grapefruit (you can discard the remaining peel). Pour all of the juice, including the lemon juice, into a large saucepan set over medium heat, and add the peel and water. Cover and bring to a boil. Take off the lid, reduce the heat to low, and simmer for 2 hours.

Add the sugar and Campari and stir to dissolve the sugar. Let the mixture continue to gently boil for 45 to 60 minutes. Monitor the marmalade and stir frequently, as it will rise quite high as it boils. Dip a wooden spoon into the marmalade, remove it, and carefully run your finger across the back of the spoon. If the finger mark stays visible, the marmalade is ready. If not, keep boiling, stirring occasionally, for another 5 to 6 minutes and repeat the test. When the marmalade is done, remove the saucepan from the heat and let it cool for 5 to 8 minutes before discarding any scum or foam visible on the surface.

Sterilize enough jars and lids to fit the marmalade (see Tip, page 69). Pour the marmalade into the sterilized jars and screw on the lid. The marmalade will thicken as it cools. If kept in a dark cool place undisturbed and unopened, the marmalade will keep for months. Opened jars stored in the fridge will keep for 7 to 10 days.

spring

M R DARCY, FROM THE NOVEL, *Pride and Prejudice* by Jane Austen, didn't come wandering into my life across the field one misty spring morning, as I'd perhaps envisioned before moving to this charming little town in the English countryside. Instead, for perhaps the first moment in my life, I took the time to dig deeply into myself, and deeply into cooking.

It rained often that first spring in England, and I spent the days at home warming up in front of the open fireplace in the living room with a cup of tea, or dressed in my mother's apron, stirring a simmering pot of soup or stew bubbling on the stove.

I cooked for one. I cooked to heal my heart, and to escape into a world of comforting flavors, familiar spices perfuming my little cottage. I also cooked for tomorrow. I cooked for everyone I wanted to gather around my future dining room table, for friends old and new, and to rediscover my roots. But perhaps most of all I cooked for myself, for the woman I wanted to become.

Exploring the familiar and discovering the new during those first months all alone in my new hometown created the perfect cocktail for growth, and the most wonderful, stable foundation on which to build.

I HAD YEARNED FOR THIS PEACEFUL QUIET LIFE, where I could hear my own heartbeat after almost twelve years of living in various cities around the world. It was not easy. The countryside felt quiet. In the absence of the buzz and noise of a bustling metropolis, I was left to listen to my own voice, or rather to learn to pay attention to that whisper that guides us on this journey through life—whether we hear it or not. I wanted to learn to listen to my own thoughts, to wake up daily to a slower pace of living.

I'd been wanting a dog for a while, but, because I was still traveling so much for work, it was the absolute wrong time to get one. My cottage and the surrounding rolling hills practically begged for a four-legged addition, though, and for an excuse to venture outside. The hills were clothed in bright green, the market in town was bustling with life and fresh spring produce, and on the twenty-seventh of April I brought home a white eighteen-month-old male rescue dog.

I'd actually spotted his rather sad face online a few weeks earlier, between speaking at a design conference in Norway and teaching a food and photography workshop in Ireland. With just a couple of images to go by, I knew we'd get along. He had that cheeky old spark in his eyes that is the recipe for both disaster and adventure. I made a plan then and there to pay him a visit upon returning to England and to adjust my work life to fit in with my personal life, rather than the other way around. It was a bold move, but one I was ready to take. So I leapt, hoping I'd find solutions as I walked this path.

Mr. Darcy may not have come wandering into my life as I had secretly hoped, but instead I got Benny—whose name I quickly changed to Mr. Whiskey—an adorable young English Pointer. He barked at me when I asked him politely to return to his basket. He ran away. He chased the neighbor's cows and chewed up my grandmother's sofa when I left him home alone. Clearly we needed some time to get to know each other, Mr. Whiskey and I, but we never gave up on each other, and luckily over time we forged a deep friendship, unlike anything I could have ever envisioned.

Yet as life was adjusting, I still felt uneasy and uncertain about the future. On one of my weekly phone calls home, I spilled my heart to my mother. "Why don't things work out the way I had hoped? I've followed my heart, haven't I?" I could feel it in my toes that moving here was the right thing to do, but it wasn't all coming together the way I had envisioned. I clutched the phone as if it were a lifeline. I still felt alone and small in this big world.

My mother paused before replying. I could tell that all she wanted to do was hug me and tell me it was all going to work out. Instead she said, "It will all come together, but not when you need it to. Work on your house, join the local choir, and take one thing at the time. And do yourself a favor and make my sour cream porridge for supper tonight. You'll know why."

She knew that with the first spoonful of this soothing and silky-smooth dish with its familiar smells of warm milk, sugar, and cinnamon, I'd find comfort. I admit that I may have teared up a little eating it, but as soon as I set down my bowl and spoon, I said out loud, "Get to work!" And so I did. With newfound dedication, I promised myself that I would steadily move forward and trust in the journey. I would learn to be grateful for what I had now and not weep for what was not yet there. Answers aren't readily available when we feel our most vulnerable and lost, but they emerge slowly and quietly as we continue to walk the road we set out on.

So, come sun or rain, ferocious winds, and bone chilling cold, Mr. Whiskey and I went about our daily adventures through town and the nearby rolling hills. I inhaled deep breaths of change and felt like each day one more piece of the puzzle fell into place, as I began to hear that inner voice that had eluded me during my twenties.

SPRING IN THE COUNTRYSIDE means the return of wild garlic. Right before the bluebells cover the grounds in the woods, it emerges, covering the grounds surrounding my cottage. We didn't have this herb where I grew up in Norway. Unfamiliar with what to do with it, yet eager to preserve its beautifully gentle aroma, I took inspiration from my time in Italy and made pesto, heaping jars of it. Experimenting with different nuts and cheeses, I quickly found my favorite: classic pine nut and olive oil with a gentle Pecorino cheese from Sicilia seemed to become the best of friends when combined.

My cottage kitchen became a production line of pesto and pickled garlic flower buds. When the white flower heads bloomed a few weeks after they first emerged, I dried them in the oven to preserve them as a spice, or tossed them fresh in my salad for an extra kick. Seasons are fleeting, and even if I simply cannot eat another pasta with wild garlic pesto by the end of one, I begin yearning for its return as soon as the first signs of the next spring emerge. This ever-changing cycle of coming and going, the ebb and flow of a year, keeps me on my toes as I enjoy the current moment while anticipating the next. This is to me what seasonal cooking is all about, making the most of what is— celebrating the flame and not mourning the ashes.

STARTERS AND SIDES

Baked Mont d'Or with
Honeycomb and Garlic

Garden Nettle Soup

Kale and Almond Soup

Creamy Cabbage Stew

Arancini with Camembert

Rosemary Breadsticks with
Herb and Carrot Butter

Braided Zopf Bread

MAINS

Taleggio and Potato Pizza

Zucchini Pasta with Pancetta
and Wild Garlic

Easter Star Anise Leg of Lamb

Risotto Milanese

Marie's Meatballs with Parsnip
and Cardamom Puree

Fennel and Potato Soup

Jansons' Potato Casserole
with Quail Eggs

DESSERTS

Ruby-Red Rhubarb Soup

Primrose and Passion Fruit
Eton Mess

Norwegian Apple Trifle

My Grandmother's No-Bake
Chocolate Biscuit Slice

Caramel Popcorn

DRINKS

Rhubarb Lemonade

Brandy Hot Chocolate
with Cardamom

BAKED MONT D'OR WITH HONEYCOMB AND GARLIC

Serves 4

Mont d'Or is a mature cheese that I often bake with garlic and rosemary when friends are coming over for drinks and nibbles, or when I want a quickly made starter that my guests can tuck into while I finish up dinner preparations in the kitchen. Baked cheese is a social dish that everyone can dive into together. As much as I adore a good Camembert, when my cheesemonger in Shaftesbury introduced me to Mont d'Or, which has a much bolder flavor, I was hooked. Garnished with sweet honeycomb filled with golden honey, when baked this cheese becomes a wonderful sweet and savory treat. Serve with Rosemary Breadsticks (page 92), slices of my No-Knead Country Loaf (page 32), or your favorite crackers. Although I truly enjoy my cheese with red wine, this one is also very good with a chilled Zinfandel.

1 Mont d'Or cheese

2 garlic cloves, quartered

2 fresh rosemary sprigs (optional)

Raw honeycomb, for serving

Bread or crackers, for serving

Preheat the oven to 180° C / 350°F.

Place the cheese in an ovenproof ramekin that's slightly bigger and taller than the cheese itself, or leave it in its wooden case. Pierce the top of the cheese with the garlic and rosemary, if desired. Place the cheese in the middle of the oven and bake until soft, 8 to 10 minutes.

Serve immediately, with the honeycomb placed on top of the warm cheese, and bread or crackers on the side.

GARDEN NETTLE SOUP

Serves 4

Without fail, as soon as the snow melted in Norway in spring, nettles and dandelions would eagerly stretch their necks and pop up everywhere. They were a welcome sight after colorless months with little plant life to speak of. My mother took their arrival as an invitation to once again cook from what her garden produced, even if these two plants are often thought of as belonging to the weed world. She'd gather fresh little shoots of nettles and dandelions, mix them with some spinach, and create a nurturing soup that tasted like a mighty kick-start from winter slumber into spring. Filled with nutrients, its earthy flavor always felt like a breath of fresh air. My mother serves the soup with halved, hard-boiled eggs in each bowl. This is my version of her spring elixir, gently flavored and oh so comforting.

---

2 tablespoons salted butter

1 medium leek, cleaned well and chopped

2 celery stalks, chopped

60g / 2 ounces small spring potatoes, peeled and chopped

2 medium shallots, chopped

4 garlic cloves, finely chopped

1 to 2 teaspoon fennel seeds, coarsely ground

1L / 4¼ cups vegetable stock

2 tablespoons all-purpose flour

200ml / ¾ cup plus 1 tablespoon, water

Sea salt and coarsely ground black pepper

40g / 1½ ounces fresh early spring nettles, finely chopped

3 tablespoons sour cream, for serving

1 scallion, trimmed and sliced, for garnish

Olive oil, for drizzling

In a large saucepan set over medium heat, melt the butter. Add the leek, celery, potatoes, shallots, garlic, and fennel seeds. Cover and cook, stirring occasionally, until soft, 10 to 12 minutes. The potatoes will still be quite hard.

In a separate medium saucepan set over medium heat, warm the stock. Add the stock to the vegetable mixture. Bring the soup to a gentle boil.

In a small bowl, stir together the flour and water, or shake it in a liquid-tight container until completely dissolved. Add the flour mixture to the soup and stir well. Reduce the heat to low and simmer until the potatoes are cooked through, about 10 minutes. Season with salt and pepper. Add the nettles and cook for 2 to 3 minutes before whizzing it all together with an immersion-blender (or working in batches in a regular blender).

Serve warm topped with a spoonful of sour cream, sliced scallions, a drizzle of olive oil, and pepper.

TIP: Make sure to use only early spring nettles, before they have bloomed and gone coarse, as older nettles will not yield the same fresh flavor.

KALE AND ALMOND SOUP

Serves 4 to 6

Although we had kale in our meals growing up, it never really enjoyed the limelight quite like it does today. It's a nourishing plant that can withstand the harsher winds during winter, and is an excellent ingredient that tides me over from winter to spring with ease. Inspired by my father's love of a healthy lifestyle, I wanted to surprise him with a soup he'd really approve of when he and my mother came to visit one cold and dreary January to take care of Mr. Whiskey while I went to Italy for work. My father smiled at me as he looked up from his bowl of green goodness and exclaimed, "It even tastes good!" Creamy with a nice crunch, this soup is lovely with a crisp white wine.

1 tablespoon salted butter

4 garlic cloves, thinly sliced

400g / 5 cups green kale, tough stems and ribs removed, leaves finely chopped

2 large potatoes, peeled and chopped

1 celery stalk, finely chopped

20g / ¼ cup almond flakes / slivered almonds

2 fresh rosemary sprigs, leaves finely chopped

1½L / 6⅓ cups vegetable stock

50g / ½ cup almond flour

200ml / ¾ cup plus 1 tablespoon double cream / heavy cream

Sea salt and coarsely ground black pepper

4 tablespoons olive oil, for drizzling

Chili oil (optional), for drizzling

In a large skillet set over medium heat, melt the butter. Add the garlic, kale, potatoes, and celery, and cook until the kale wilts and the celery begins to soften, 6 to 8 minutes. Set aside.

In a small skillet set over low heat, lightly toast the almond flakes with half of the chopped rosemary until fragrant, 3 to 4 minutes. Set aside.

In a medium saucepan set over medium heat, warm the stock. Add the almond flour and the remaining rosemary, and stir well. Add the kale mixture, bring to a simmer over low heat, and cook until the potatoes are tender, 10 to 15 minutes. Using an immersion blender (or working in batches in a regular blender), blend the soup, then push it through a fine-mesh sieve into a serving bowl. Add the cream and season to taste with salt and pepper.

Serve the soup warm with a drizzle of olive oil or chili oil, if desired, and a sprinkle of the toasted almond flakes.

CREAMY CABBAGE STEW

STUET KÅL

Serves 4 to 6

Cabbage is perhaps quite an unassuming vegetable. Yet who would have thought it could be so aromatic and flavorful when paired with nutmeg in a creamy white sauce and left to stew away? My mother has made this cabbage stew as a side for meat dishes ever since I was a little girl, and I still prefer it that way. In particular, I think it's wonderful served with a good steak or Norwegian Pork Belly (page 39), though my favorite is perhaps alongside Marie's Meatballs (page 113). A little goes a long way, and after you've made this once, you'll want to make it again and again. Perhaps I should rename this recipe "My Mother's Ode to the Cabbage"!

1L / 4¼ cups water

½ head (about 700g / 1 pound) white cabbage, cut into bite-size pieces

3½ tablespoons salted butter

50g / ⅓ cup all-purpose flour

1 teaspoon ground nutmeg

500ml / 2 cups plus 2 tablespoons whole milk

Sea salt and ground white pepper

In a medium saucepan set over medium-high heat, bring the water to a boil. Add the cabbage and boil until tender, 15 to 20 minutes.

Meanwhile, in a separate medium saucepan set over medium heat, melt the butter. Add the flour, nutmeg, and milk and season to taste with salt and pepper. Cook, stirring constantly, until thickened, 10 to 15 minutes.

Drain the cabbage, add it to the sauce, and stir well. Serve hot.

ARANCINI WITH CAMEMBERT

Makes 18 to 20 arancini

When I studied fashion design in Milan in my early twenties, I was introduced to the famous, golden, saffron-based Risotto Milanese. Remaking this favorite risotto of mine, I always end up with lots left over. Perhaps my eyes are bigger than my belly. But I'm not the only one, and the Italians have of course come up with a delicious solution to this little problem: *arancini*, which are deep-fried balls of leftover risotto stuffed with cheese. I like to use Camembert, as the flavors work well with the risotto, but you can use your favorite melting cheese.

1L / 4¼ cups vegetable oil for deep-frying

4 medium eggs

½ batch Risotto Milanese (page 108), chilled

100g / ½ cup ground almonds

160g / 1¼ cups all-purpose flour

140g / 1 cup bread crumbs

120g / 4 ounces Camembert, diced

In a large saucepan set over medium heat, heat the oil until it reaches 180°C / 350°F.

In a large bowl, beat 2 of the eggs. Add the risotto, ground almonds, and 30g / ¼ cup of flour and mix well.

Spread the remaining flour on a plate. In a medium bowl, beat the remaining eggs. Sprinkle the bread crumbs onto a deep plate. Arrange the dishes side by side, in the order of flour, eggs, and bread crumbs. Dip your fingers into a bowl of water and form the risotto mixture into golf ball–size pieces. Using your finger, push a hole into the center of each ball and insert 2 or 3 cubes of Camembert. Wrap the risotto around the cheese to seal it completely. Carefully roll each ball first in the flour, then in the egg, and finally in the bread crumbs.

Check that the oil has reached its frying temperature of 180°C / 350°F by dropping in a bread crumb. It should sizzle away and quickly turn golden. Line a plate with paper towels and set it beside the pan of oil.

Working in batches, carefully lower 2 or 3 risotto balls into the oil and deep-fry until golden and crispy, 2 to 3 minutes. Using a slotted spoon, transfer the arancini to the paper towel–lined plate to drain. Repeat with the remaining risotto balls. Serve warm.

ROSEMARY BREADSTICKS
WITH HERB AND CARROT BUTTER

Makes 15 to 20 breadsticks

All the way through Europe on our many road trips growing up, I'd snack on *grissini*, which are Italian breadsticks. They have little flavoring save salt and olive oil, yet they are a treasured favorite. Passing by aqueducts, old cathedrals, overgrown rivers, through field after field, wonky old towns and cities as we traveled from France to Norway, I'd constantly nibble away. As I grew older, my mother began baking her own variations, adding whatever herbs were in season in her garden. I love to serve these with my mother's herb and carrot butter for dipping, and they're also a lovely accompaniment for soups. They will keep for two to three days, but are best on the day they're baked.

320g / 2½ cups all-purpose flour, plus additional for kneading

½ teaspoon sea salt

2 teaspoons active dry yeast

250ml / 1 cup whole milk

2 tablespoons olive oil

Salted butter, for greasing

200g / 1⅓ cups salted butter, melted, for brushing

30g / ¼ cup finely chopped fresh rosemary

Flaky sea salt and coarsely ground black pepper

Herb and Carrot Butter (recipe follows), for serving

In a large bowl, combine the flour, salt, and yeast.

In a small saucepan set over medium heat, warm the milk to 37°C / 95°F. Test a drop on the back of your hand; it should feel the same temperature as your skin. Add the oil. Make a well in the flour mixture, add the warm milk, and combine well. Place the dough on a flat surface and knead for 10 to 15 minutes, adding a sprinkle more of flour or water if needed, until the dough is firm yet tender. Cover with a kitchen towel and let rest in a warm, draft-free place until doubled in size, 1 to 1½ hours.

Butter a large baking sheet that's big enough to fit your breadsticks.

On a lightly floured surface, divide the dough into 2 equal parts. Knead each for 3 to 5 minutes, adding more flour if needed, until you have a firm yet

recipe continues

smooth dough. Using a rolling pin, roll each piece into a 1½- to 2-centimeter / about ½-inch-thick rectangle. Brush the melted butter on the dough, setting aside a small amount to brush on the dough right before baking. Generously sprinkle the rosemary, salt, and pepper over the dough. Cut the dough lengthwise into 2 to 3 centimeter / about 1-inch-wide strips. Twist the strips into a spiraled breadstick and place on the prepared baking sheet, leaving room for them to rise. Brush with the remaining melted butter and season with more salt and pepper, if desired. Cover the baking sheet with a kitchen towel and let rise for 15 to 20 minutes in a warm, draft-free place.

Preheat the oven to 200°C / 400°F.

Bake the breadsticks until lightly golden, 10 to 15 minutes. Let cool slightly before serving with the herb and carrot butter.

HERB AND CARROT BUTTER

Makes about 250g / 1 cup

250g / 1 cup salted butter, room temperature	2 tablespoons finely chopped fresh chives	½ teaspoon sea salt
2 tablespoons cold water	½ teaspoon finely chopped fresh mint	¼ teaspoon coarsely ground black pepper
2 tablespoons finely chopped carrot	¼ teaspoon curry powder	Calendula flower, or any other edible flower, for garnish (optional)

In a small bowl, use a spatula to beat the butter until it is light and white in color, 2 to 3 minutes. Add the water and stir well. Add the carrots, chives, mint, curry powder, salt, and pepper. Mix well. Garnish with edible flowers, if desired.

BRAIDED ZOPF BREAD

Makes 2 standard loaves

When I was fifteen and sixteen, I spent my summers in Switzerland. Buying bread from the bakeries in Zurich and Bern, I discovered *zopf,* a delightful braided white loaf that I've re-created wherever I've lived ever since. There are many beautiful ways to braid a loaf, but I like to do it the same way I fix my hair, with three parts, tucking in each end of the bread to hide the ends. It emerges so temptingly golden from the oven, it's best enjoyed the day it's baked.

900g / 6⅔ cups strong bread
    flour, plus more for kneading

1 teaspoon sea salt

150g / 9 tablespoons salted butter,
    cut into small pieces, room
    temperature

1 medium egg, lightly beaten

500ml / 2 cups plus 2 tablespoons
    whole milk

5 teaspoons active dry yeast

Pinch of sugar

Vegetable oil, for greasing

1 egg yolk, beaten, for brushing

In a large bowl, sift together the flour and salt. Using your fingers, work in the butter until well combined. Stir in the egg.

In a small saucepan set over low heat, heat the milk until lukewarm. Remove the pan from the heat and whisk in the yeast and sugar. Add the milk mixture to the flour mixture and stir to combine. Transfer the dough to a cool work surface, dust with flour, and knead until smooth and elastic, 15 to 20 minutes. Brush the bowl with oil and place the dough back into it. Cover and let rise in a warm, draft-free place for 2 hours, until almost doubled in size.

Put the dough on a floured work surface and knead for another minute before dividing it into 2 pieces. Cut each piece into 3 smaller pieces, shaping each into a 25- to 28-centimeter- / 10- to 11-inch-long rope. Take 3 of the ropes and braid them together, tucking the ends underneath. Repeat with the remaining 3 ropes. Let the loaves rise for another 30 minutes.

Preheat the oven to 180°C / 350°F.

Line a large baking sheet with parchment paper, place the loaves on it, and brush with the beaten egg yolk. Bake for 15 minutes, then cover with foil and bake until golden brown and cooked through, about 20 more minutes.

TALEGGIO AND POTATO PIZZA

Makes 2 pizzas

When the snow melts and the earth thaws, spring potatoes begin appearing at the market in my new hometown. With skins soft enough to be left on after a gentle rinse, and a sweetness to their aroma, these potatoes are a particular favorite of mine. We had them in my childhood home, too, where my mother would quickly boil them and serve them with a dollop of butter, a sprinkle of salt, and fresh parsley. She'd put them in salads and on the breakfast table with sour cream and pickled herring. On one of her first visits to my new cottage, after spotting these humble little vegetables at the local greengrocer, she suggested making a potato pizza. We loved it! I made a few more over the next few weeks, adding this and subtracting that until I settled on this version, which uses Taleggio, one of my favorite cheeses. Serve with a chilled dry cider.

Pizza Dough (recipe follows)

200g / 6 ounces new potatoes, scrubbed and thinly sliced

4 tablespoons truffle oil

4 to 5 medium shallots, thinly sliced

1 to 2 garlic cloves, finely chopped

3 to 4 tablespoons water

300g / 10 ounces Taleggio, chopped

Sea salt and coarsely ground black pepper

80g / 3 ounces pecorino, grated

4 teaspoons fresh rosemary leaves, roughly chopped

2 tablespoons olive oil

Bake the pizza dough according to the recipe directions.

Preheat the oven to 175°C / 350°F.

Place the potato slices in a medium saucepan, cover with water, and bring to a simmer over medium-low heat. Cook until tender, 4 to 6 minutes. Drain the potatoes in a colander and set aside.

Return the saucepan to medium-low heat and add ½ tablespoon of the truffle oil. Add the shallots and garlic, and cook, stirring, for 2 to 3 minutes. Add the water and allow the mixture to cook for 2 to 3 more minutes, stirring occasionally to avoid burning.

Spread the shallot and garlic mixture in a thin layer over the pizza crusts. Top with a layer of potato slices, and scatter the Taleggio over the potatoes.

recipe continues

Season to taste with salt and pepper before sprinkling with the pecorino and rosemary. Drizzle with the olive oil.

Bake until the cheese is bubbling but hasn't browned yet, 8 to 10 minutes. Drizzle the remaining truffle oil over the pizzas and serve hot.

PIZZA DOUGH

Makes 2 pizza crusts

After baking the pizza crusts, top the pizza base with anything you please. Or serve them plain with extra olive oil and fresh herbs as flatbreads.

450g / 3⅓ cups all-purpose flour, plus more for dusting	1 teaspoon sugar	2 tablespoons olive oil
1½ teaspoons sea salt	1 teaspoon active dry yeast	250ml / 1 cup lukewarm water

In a large bowl, combine the flour and salt. Stir in the sugar and yeast, and make a well in the middle.

In a small bowl, combine the oil and water, then slowly pour the mixture in a thin stream into the well in the flour mixture. Slowly stir the mixture until it comes together as a dough. On a smooth work surface, knead until the dough is smooth and elastic, 10 to 15 minutes.

Sprinkle some flour in the large bowl, place the dough back in the bowl, and cover with a damp kitchen towel. Let rise in a warm, draft-free place until doubled in size, 1 to 2 hours.

Place a pizza stone (or large baking sheet) in the oven and preheat to 200°C / 400°F.

On a lightly floured work surface, divide the dough in half and form each section into a ball. Using a rolling pin, roll out 2 disks the size of your pizza stone or baking sheet.

Remove the pizza stone or baking sheet from the oven, lightly flour, and arrange the dough on top. Drizzle the dough with olive oil. Return to the oven and bake until golden and crisp, 8 to 10 minutes.

ZUCCHINI PASTA WITH PANCETTA
AND WILD GARLIC

Serves 2

With a basket hanging from my arm and wellies on my feet, I spend my April days gathering wild garlic. I pickle the budding flowers, make pesto from its narrow green leaves, and make the most of this hardy plant by also harvesting the fully opened flowers, and drying them in the oven for 10 to 15 minutes or sprinkling them over green salads and omelets. There are endless possibilities for using this versatile plant, whose mild garlic flavor I crave as spring arrives and the forest ground awakens from slumber. It always seems like the wild garlic season will last forever, with the elongated leaves covering every inch between the trees surrounding my cottage, yet before I know it I find myself rushing to blend batches of pesto before the garlic is gone with the change of seasons. You can freeze the pesto, should you wish to extend the season even longer. Spread on toast or freshly baked bread, or tossed in this pasta dish, this pesto deliciously sings the praise of the humble wild plant that many simply stomp over without thinking about its great culinary possibilities.

200g / 7 ounces spaghetti

200g / 2 cups diced slab pancetta

½ tablespoon olive oil

2 to 3 tablespoons pine nuts

1 courgette / zucchini, unpeeled

5 to 6 tablespoons Wild Garlic Pesto (recipe follows) or basil pesto

Freshly grated Parmesan, for serving

In a medium saucepan of boiling salted water, cook the spaghetti according to the package instructions until al dente. Drain, reserving 2 tablespoons of the pasta water.

In a small skillet set over medium heat, fry the pancetta in the oil until it is crisp and golden, 8 to 10 minutes. Transfer to a plate and set aside. Reduce the heat to medium-low, add the pine nuts, and cook, stirring frequently, until toasted, 3 to 5 minutes. Transfer to the plate with the pancetta.

Cut the ends off the zucchini. Using a spiralizer, cut the zucchini into long

recipe continues

noodle-like strands. Put the zucchini noodles into the skillet and cook over medium-low heat, stirring, until heated through, 2 to 3 minutes. Add the spaghetti.

In a small bowl, combine the pesto with the reserved pasta water. Stir the pesto, pancetta, and pine nuts into the spaghetti and zucchini and toss to combine. Serve immediately with a sprinkling of grated Parmesan cheese.

TIP: If desired, you can make this recipe using only the spaghetti, omitting the zucchini. Or you can do the opposite, using just the zucchini spirals; you'll need to add 2 more zucchini to the original recipe.

WILD GARLIC PESTO

Makes 500ml / 2¼ cups

Serve this with the preceding zucchini and pasta recipe, or anywhere else you would use pesto.

2 teaspoons coarsely ground black pepper	100g / 3¼ ounces fresh spinach, washed well and drained	50ml / scant ¼ cup olive oil
40g / 1½ ounces pecorino, grated	50g / 2 ounces wild garlic leaves	½ teaspoon crushed red pepper flakes
40g / 1½ ounces Parmesan, grated	60g / ½ cup pine nuts	2 teaspoons sea salt

In a blender, blend together the pepper, pecorino, Parmesan, spinach, garlic leaves, pine nuts, oil, red pepper flakes, and salt until it reaches a creamy consistency. If storing, sterilize 1 or 2 jars (see Tip, page 69), depending on the size of the jars. Pour the pesto into the jar(s) and refrigerate. This is best consumed on the day it's made, though it will keep in the fridge for up to 1 week.

EASTER STAR ANISE
LEG OF LAMB

Serves 6

At midnight, right before winter gave way to spring, there would often be light glowing from our little red barn on the small farm where I grew up. One evening wintery storms swept through the courtyard, and my mother woke me up in the middle of the night. As we hurried out the front door to the barn, grabbing warm coats on the way, we could see our breath in the cold. My mother had woken me up because my father was away on a business trip, and there had been hints that the first lambs from our little flock of sheep would be born that night. Sure enough, a ewe carrying twins was about to give birth for the very first time. There we stood, mother and daughter side by side. Due to my young age, I was of little help, but I watched in awe as my mother rolled up the sleeves of her long nightgown and reached for the lamb that seemed to be having trouble with its launch into the world. My heart was pounding as I saw steam coming up from the firstborn lying on the straw, the ewe licking her clean. Witnessing new life being born always fills me with the same awe. Being so close to the circle of life made me truly appreciate every cut of the animal and all that our garden and surrounding hedges would yield.

I've spent almost as many Easters without my mother's traditional celebratory cooking as I have with it. Like many other families, on Easter Sunday we would gather around a candlelit table set with a leg of lamb that had been roasted with rosemary and garlic. One recent Easter, I stood in my own kitchen here in the English countryside and missed the familiar traditions. I wanted to fill my house with the smells of my childhood home, yet instead of reaching for garlic and rosemary, I found myself yearning for star anise and white wine. I realized I was about to put down roots, culinary roots, of my very own. I invited friends over for a taste, and it was a hit. Serve with a hearty red wine and Roast Potatoes (page 107).

recipe continues

1 tablespoon olive oil, plus more for the meat

2 medium yellow onions, chopped

2 carrots, chopped

9 whole star anise

1 garlic head, halved, plus 10 cloves, halved

2 to 3 fresh rosemary sprigs

2 to 3 fresh thyme sprigs

2 dried bay leaves

1.8kg / 4 pounds leg of lamb, on the bone

Sea salt and coarsely ground black pepper

½ tablespoon salted butter

120ml / ½ cup white wine, plus more for basting

Preheat the oven to 120°C / 250°F.

In a large Dutch oven or an ovenproof dish, with a lid, heat the oil over medium. Add the onion, carrot, and 4 star anise and cook, stirring, until golden, 4 to 5 minutes. Add the halved garlic head, rosemary, thyme, and bay leaves and cook for 5 minutes. Transfer the vegetables and herbs to a plate. Save any liquid for stock and wipe the pot clean.

Liberally massage the lamb with oil and season with salt and pepper. Using a sharp knife, make 20 small cuts into the meat. Break the remaining star anise into small pieces. Insert half a garlic clove into each cut, followed by a piece of anise.

Place the Dutch oven over high heat and melt the butter. Add the lamb and cook until lightly browned, 4 to 5 minutes, making sure to turn it so all sides are browned. Transfer the meat to a plate. Add the wine to the pot and scrape up any browned bits on the bottom of the pan. Return the vegetables to the pot and set the leg of lamb on top. Cover tightly and place in the oven.

Roast, basting every 30 minutes or so with the remaining wine and the sauce forming in the bottom of the Dutch oven, until the meat is falling off the bone, 4 to 5 hours. Transfer the lamb to a plate or cutting board and let it rest for 10 minutes. Transfer the vegetables to a serving platter; discard the thyme and rosemary sprigs and the bay leaves. Arrange the lamb on top of the vegetables. Tent with foil to keep warm.

Pour any remaining liquid from the bottom of the Dutch oven into a medium saucepan. Set the pan over medium heat and simmer until reduced by half, 4 to 6 minutes. Strain the gravy and serve alongside the meat and vegetables.

ROAST POTATOES

Serves 6 to 8

Crunchy and golden, this classic English potato recipe has a few variations, but this is my go-to version. To me, duck fat is essential, as it both enhances the flavor and the overall crunch; however, goose fat or olive oil can be used instead. Almost every Sunday during winter, I serve a roast with a side of these potatoes, but once you've discovered something so simple and good as roast potatoes, there's no reason to limit yourself to only serving them with your Sunday roast. They work wonderfully as a side for any dish that you typically pair with potatoes.

1kg / 2.2 pounds potatoes, peeled and chopped

100g / 6 tablespoons duck fat

Sea salt and coarsely ground black pepper

6 to 8 sprigs rosemary, leaves finely chopped

100g / 1 cup freshly grated Parmesan

Preheat the oven to 180°C / 350°F.

Place the potatoes in a large saucepan and cover with cold water. Bring to a boil over high heat and cook until parboiled, 6 to 8 minutes. Drain and then shake them roughly in a colander to remove excess water.

Place a roasting pan large enough to hold all the potatoes in a single layer in the oven to preheat for 5 minutes. Remove from oven and spread the duck fat over the bottom of the pan. Pour the potatoes into the roasting pan and stir well to ensure all the potatoes are covered with the fat. Season with salt and pepper to taste and stir well.

Bake for 25 to 30 minutes. Remove the potatoes from the oven and sprinkle with the rosemary and Parmesan. Shake or stir thoroughly to ensure each potato is well coated. Bake until the potatoes are crisp and lightly brown, 20 to 30 minutes more.

RISOTTO MILANESE

Serves 4

One of my favorite traditional restaurants in Milan is Al Matarel, which is right off Corso Garibaldi, just a stone's throw from where I lived while studying fashion design in my twenties. It's a family-run place whose owners scribble with a marker on their window when the Alba truffle has arrived, an event that always made my heart skip. This is where I first had Risotto Milanese, a traditional saffron and bone marrow–based risotto that's golden, creamy, and ever so tasty. During those few months when the Alba truffle was at its peak, I'd order my risotto with a generous shaving on top as a luxurious treat, but with or without the addition of truffle, it is simply glorious.

1½L / 6⅓ cups chicken stock

3 tablespoons salted butter

½ yellow onion, finely chopped

3½ tablespoons beef bone marrow

400g / 2 cups Arborio or Carnaroli rice

100ml / ⅓ cup plus 1 tablespoon dry white wine

1 tablespoon saffron, finely ground

Sea salt

80g / 1 cup freshly grated Parmesan

Coarsely ground black pepper

In a medium saucepan set over medium-low heat, warm the stock.

In a separate large saucepan set over medium heat, melt 1½ tablespoons of butter. Add the onion and sauté, stirring, 2 to 3 minutes. Add the bone marrow and continue to sauté for 3 to 4 minutes until well combined. Add the rice and cook, stirring, until the rice is completely coated with the fat and is translucent, about 2 minutes. Add the wine and cook, stirring, until the liquid has evaporated, 2 to 3 minutes.

Reduce the heat to medium-low and add 2 ladles of the warm stock to the rice mixture. Cook, stirring gently at regular intervals, until the stock is completely absorbed, 4 to 6 minutes, monitoring it so the rice doesn't dry out. Repeat with 2 ladles of stock at a time, continually monitoring the rice and stirring regularly, until the rice cannot absorb any more stock, 15 to 20 minutes, and has a loose, creamy consistency.

In a small bowl, combine the ground saffron with half a ladle of stock, stirring to dissolve the saffron completely. Gently stir the saffron into the rice mixture. Taste the rice and season with salt. Simmer until the stock is absorbed, yet the rice is still tender, 1 to 2 minutes. The rice should be al dente. If needed, add more stock, half a ladle at a time.

Add 60g / ¾ cup of Parmesan and the remaining 1½ tablespoons of butter to the rice, and stir until the butter is melted. Cover the risotto for a minute before serving with a sprinkle of the remaining grated Parmesan and a couple grinds of pepper.

MARIE'S MEATBALLS WITH PARSNIP AND CARDAMOM PUREE

Makes 30 small meatballs

"Just one more!" I'd beg with a grin on my face as my mother browned innumerable meatballs in a hissing skillet. When I was able to slip one from the cast-iron skillet, I felt like I had snatched the ultimate snack. This recipe, a true childhood favorite, is such an easy dinner to make, and can be made in advance. Filled to the brim with some of my most-used spices, these meatballs have a distinct Scandinavian flair. Traditionally, they're simply served with boiled potatoes and brown gravy. My favorite way to serve them is with Parsnip and Cardamom Puree (recipe follows), Brown Gravy (page 41), Creamy Cabbage Stew (page 88), and Cranberry Sauce (recipe follows).

2 tablespoons salted butter, cubed, room temperature, plus more for greasing, frying, and buttering

500g / 1 pound ground pork

500g / 1 pound ground beef

1 yellow onion, finely chopped

65g / ⅔ cup rolled oats

4 medium eggs

1 teaspoon ground cardamom

1 teaspoon ground cumin

½ teaspoon ground cloves

½ teaspoon ground cinnamon

1 to 2 teaspoons sea salt

¼ teaspoon coarsely ground black pepper

Parsnip and Cardamom Puree (recipe follows), for serving

Cranberry Sauce (recipe follows), for serving

Brown Gravy (page 41), for serving

Preheat the oven to 180°C / 350°F with a rack set in the middle. Butter a large 35 × 45-centimeter / 14 × 18-inch baking dish.

In a large bowl, using a wooden spoon or your hands, combine the pork, beef, onion, oats, eggs, cubed butter, cardamom, cumin, cloves, cinnamon, salt, and pepper. Place a small bowl filled with water next to you to dip your fingers in when shaping the meatballs. Dip your fingers in the water, scoop out a little meatball mixture, and shape it into a ball about the size of a plum, 5 centimeters / 2 inches in diameter.

In a large skillet set over medium heat, melt 1 teaspoon of butter. Working in batches, add several meatballs to the pan and cook until browned and crispy

recipe continues

on all sides, 6 to 7 minutes, turning regularly. Transfer the meatballs to the prepared baking dish. Repeat with the remaining meatballs.

Bake until cooked through, 10 to 12 minutes. Take one out to test that the center is not pink before removing them from the oven. Serve warm with the parsnip puree, cranberry sauce, and brown gravy.

PARSNIP AND CARDAMOM PUREE

Serves 4

Serve hot alongside Marie's Meatballs (page 113), Norwegian Pork Belly (page 39), or any cooked meat.

---

4 tablespoons salted butter	1 teaspoon ground cardamom	Sea salt and coarsely ground black pepper
1kg / 2.2 pounds parsnips, chopped	500ml / 2 cups plus 2 tablespoons water	1 to 2 tablespoons double cream / heavy cream
1 garlic clove, finely chopped		

In a medium saucepan set over medium heat, melt the butter. Add the parsnips, garlic, and cardamom and cook until tender, 5 to 10 minutes. Add the water, bring to a boil, and boil for 20 to 25 minutes, until the parsnips are completely soft, checking regularly and adding more water if needed so the mixture doesn't dry out. Season with salt and pepper. Using an immersion blender (or working in batches in a regular blender), puree until smooth. Stir in 1 tablespoon of cream, adding more if the puree is too thick.

CRANBERRY SAUCE

Serves 4

500g / 4 cups fresh or frozen cranberries

250g / 2 cups sugar

1 cinnamon stick

1 tablespoon salted butter

450ml / scant 2 cups water

In a medium saucepan set over medium heat, combine all the ingredients and bring to a boil. Reduce the heat to low and simmer until it reaches a thin, sauce-like consistency, 12 to 15 minutes. Discard the cinnamon stick.

The sauce will keep in an airtight container in the refrigerator for 7 to 10 days. Serve at room temperature.

FENNEL AND POTATO SOUP

Serves 4

With its mild anise flavor, fennel is right up there among my favorite vegetables. Perhaps this is where my true Scandinavian colors shine through—my love for licorice and everything anise-flavored is endless. This quiet and soothing soup is a lovely starter on a warm spring day. Serve with freshly ground pepper and a drizzle of olive oil on top, paired with a crisp dry white wine.

---

2 tablespoons olive oil, plus more for serving

3 tablespoons unsalted butter

300g / 10 ounces fennel bulbs (about 2 bulbs), coarsely chopped

½ large yellow onion, coarsely chopped

½ celery stalk, coarsely chopped

2 garlic cloves, finely chopped

4 anise seeds, coarsely ground

1 teaspoon fennel seeds, crushed

800ml / 3⅓ cups vegetable stock

200g / 7 ounces potatoes, peeled and cubed

120ml / ½ cup double cream / heavy cream, plus more for serving (optional)

Sea salt and finely ground black pepper

In a large saucepan set over medium-high heat, heat 1 tablespoon of olive oil and 2 tablespoons of butter. Add the fennel, onion, celery, garlic, anise seeds, and fennel seeds and cook, stirring occasionally, until soft, 5 minutes. Transfer the vegetables to a plate.

Add 2 tablespoons of vegetable stock to the pan and cook for 2 to 3 minutes, scraping up any browned bits on the bottom of the pan. Add the potatoes and the remaining tablespoon of butter and cook until tender, 5 minutes, before adding the remaining stock. Bring to a boil, reduce the heat to medium-low, and cook until the potatoes are soft, 10 to 15 minutes. Add the fennel and onion mixture and the cream and continue to simmer until well combined and soft, 5 minutes more.

Using an immersion blender (or working in batches in a regular blender), puree the soup until smooth. Season to taste with salt. If the soup is too thick, add some boiling water to thin it out.

Serve hot with a dash of cream, if desired, a drizzle of olive oil, and finely ground pepper sprinkled on top.

JANSONS' POTATO CASSEROLE
WITH QUAIL EGGS

FRISTELSE

Serves 4

My mother told me that this family recipe is borrowed from the Swedes. Topped with anchovies, it's a lovely salty, creamy, and hearty potato-based dish that is wonderfully rich and filling. On weekends when the spring sun has yet to warm up the rolling hills around the cottage, I often make this for lunch before setting off on a long walk with my dog, Mr. Whiskey. I also sometimes divide it into smaller portions, as I've accounted for in this recipe, and serve it as a warm starter before a lighter main course.

---

1 teaspoon unsalted butter, plus more for greasing

2 yellow onions, cut into thick rings

8 British Maris Piper potatoes (Yukon Gold will also work), peeled and grated

Sea salt and coarsely ground black pepper

100g / ½ cup frozen unsalted butter, grated

¼ teaspoon ground nutmeg

250ml / 1 cup double cream / heavy cream

2 tablespoons freshly grated Parmesan

10 to 12 anchovy fillets

6 quail eggs (optional)

Preheat the oven to 200°C / 400°F with a rack set in the middle.

Place a medium saucepan over low heat, and melt 1 teaspoon of butter. Add the onions and cook, stirring, until softened, 5 to 7 minutes. Set aside.

Butter a medium baking dish. Cover the bottom of the dish with a layer of grated potatoes and top with a thin layer of the onions. Season lightly with salt, but be more generous with pepper. Sprinkle half of the grated butter over the onions. Repeat the layers of potatoes, onions, seasoning, and butter, ending with a final layer of potatoes.

In a small bowl, combine the nutmeg and cream, and pour the mixture over the potato layers. Sprinkle with the Parmesan before covering the top with the anchovies.

Bake until the potatoes are completely soft and the top has a light golden crust, 25 to 30 minutes.

Serve warm with half a quail egg on each portion.

RUBY-RED RHUBARB SOUP

Serves 4

As soon as the warmth of the sun returns in the spring, rhubarb emerges from its long slumber without hesitation, shooting up like a weed. When I was a little girl, my mother would fill the bottom of a mug with a bit of sugar and attach it to my belt before I went on a wander in the garden. I'd search out the juiciest ruby-red rhubarb, peel off its skin, and dip it in the sugar. The crunch as I bit into its bitter flesh mixed with the sweetness of the sugar made me both cringe and smile with delight. During spring and summer, my mother would fill her baskets weekly to make jam, cordials, and soups with it. Served warm or cold, her rhubarb soup was something to look forward to, and I still can't get enough of it. Keep the peel on the rhubarb for a colorful soup, and enjoy with port wine.

1 vanilla bean	1 cinnamon stick	2 tablespoons cornstarch
550g / 1 pound rhubarb stalks, cut into 1cm / ⅓ inch-thick slices	500ml / 2 cups plus 3 tablespoons water	4 tablespoons plain yogurt, for serving
1 heaping teaspoon salted butter	100g / ½ cup sugar	Coarsely ground black pepper, for serving

Split the vanilla bean lengthwise and use the back of a knife to scrape the seeds into a large saucepan. Toss the vanilla bean into the pan, and add the rhubarb, butter, and cinnamon. Cover the pan and set it over medium heat. Cook, stirring occasionally, for 2 to 3 minutes. The rhubarb will yield liquid as soon as it starts to heat. Add 500ml / 2 cups of water, bring to a boil, then reduce the heat to medium-low. Let the mixture simmer until the rhubarb is completely soft, 10 to 15 minutes. Remove and discard any foam that rises to the surface. Add the sugar and carefully stir until it is dissolved, 1 to 2 minutes.

In a small bowl, dissolve the cornstarch in the remaining 3 tablespoons of water. Add the mixture to the soup. Simmer until thickened, about 5 minutes.

Remove and discard the cinnamon stick and vanilla bean before serving. Serve warm or chilled with a dollop of yogurt and a sprinkling of pepper.

PRIMROSE AND PASSION FRUIT
ETON MESS

Serves 6 to 8; makes 12 meringues

Eton mess is an English classic, and such a wonderfully easy, ever-so-tasty dessert. It consists of broken meringues, cream, and berries. Depending on the season, I use whatever fruits or berries that are ripe. And during the very cold first weeks of spring, I source the little yellow flowers of primrose that emerge and combine them with exotic passion fruit.

For weeks I'd been wanting to pick the primroses growing in sunny patches in the woods around my cottage, but time flies, as they say, and so did my very first spring in my new home. Work had me tossing and turning at night, and putting off tasks that were not on the immediate to-do list was a must. Sadly, picking primroses was bumped down the list week after week. After a long walk with Mr. Whiskey one afternoon, I met a new neighbor with a fist full of beautiful yellow primroses. "Aren't they gorgeous?" she said, and smiled at me. I could only admire her lovely little bouquet and promise myself yet again not to put it off any longer. The next morning I went out in the woods early and returned with a small basketful of these lovely bright yellow and softly scented flowers. Soon meringues were baking in the oven while I whipped cream and brought out a jar of homemade Clotted Cream (recipe follows). If you're unable to purchase or make clotted cream, substitute a full batch of My Mother's Whipped Cream (recipe follows).

4 medium egg whites

200g / 1 cup caster sugar / superfine sugar

350g / 2 cups Clotted Cream (recipe follows)

½ batch My Mother's Whipped Cream (recipe follows)

100g / ½ cup fresh passion fruit flesh, or if unavailable, store-bought passion fruit coulis

½ cup toasted pistachios (see Tip, page 125)

Handful of fresh primrose flowers

Preheat the oven to 100°C / 210°F. Line 1 or 2 rimmed baking sheets with parchment paper.

recipe continues

In a large bowl, beat the egg whites with an electric hand mixer until soft peaks form, 5 to 6 minutes. With the mixer running, gradually add the sugar until it's incorporated. Continue to beat the whites until the mixture is thick and holds stiff peaks, 4 to 10 minutes.

Spoon the meringue onto the baking sheet. Aim to form twelve 8- to 10-centimeter / 3- to 4-inch disks, keeping in mind that the diameter will enlarge as the meringues bake. The disks don't have to be perfect. (A tip for keeping the paper in place while spooning out the meringue is to add a tiny dollop of the meringue mixture underneath each corner of the paper.)

Bake the meringues until they are crisp on the outside and sound hollow when tapped on the bottom, 1½ to 2 hours, depending on the humidity. Let cool in the oven with the door slightly ajar for 1 to 1½ hours.

To assemble, break the meringues into 2 to 3 pieces and layer them in small tumblers or bowls. Top with clotted cream, whipped cream, and passion fruit coulis, and sprinkle with the toasted pistachios and fresh primroses.

TIP: The meringues can easily be made in advance, and when completely cooled, they can be stored in an airtight container for up to 2 weeks.

CLOTTED CREAM

Makes 1L / 4¼ cups

A traditional sweet delight from the UK, this spread is also delicious with Prosecco Scones (page 280) and Rosewater and Strawberry Jam (page 187).

1L / 4¼ cups double cream / heavy cream

Preheat the oven to 80°C / 175°F with a rack set in the bottom third.

Pour the cream into a 25 × 30- centimeter / 10 × 12-inch baking dish. The cream should be 5 centimeters / 2 inches high. Place the dish on the lowest rack in the oven and bake until a light golden crust forms, 8 to 10 hours.

Remove the pan from the oven and let cool in a cool place (but not the fridge) for 8 hours.

The clotted cream will keep in an airtight container in the refrigerator for 4 days.

MY MOTHER'S WHIPPED CREAM

Makes about 750ml / 3 cups

Why would I include a recipe for whipped cream, you may wonder, but, you see, whipped cream isn't always just whipped cream. Some recipes, like this one, have magic ingredients that elevate them. My mother's secret is vanilla paste and sour cream, which adds that wee hint of sour to the sweet. Try it—I hope you'll like it as much as I do.

500ml / 2 cups plus 2 tablespoons double cream / heavy cream

2 heaping tablespoons sour cream

1 tablespoon sugar

2 teaspoons vanilla paste

In a large bowl, use an electric hand mixer to beat together all the ingredients until soft peaks form. Sadly, this whipped cream does not keep and is best eaten on the day you make it.

TIP: To toast nuts, put them in a large dry skillet and cook over low heat, shaking the pan often to prevent burning, until fragrant, 3 to 4 minutes.

NORWEGIAN APPLE TRIFLE

TILSLØRTE BONDEPIKER

Serves 6

My grandmother was a wonderful hostess who was always impeccably prepared. She stored her sweet cake crumbs in an old tin box covered in chipped
paint, her whipped cream in a glass jar in the fridge, and her apple mash
on a shelf in the kitchen. After supper, she'd reach for the tin box and spoon
the whipped cream and apple mash over the cake crumbs, and *voilà,* we'd
have dessert. Although this recipe is my mother's version of this traditional
Norwegian treat, the dish makes me think of my grandmother. She was always
so enchanting during those Sunday suppers as she sat with three generations
around her dining room table, singing grace, while I cheekily kept an eye
on my brother so he wouldn't beat me to the first bowl of dessert. Easily prepared in advance, this lovely dessert tastes decadent, is gently flavored, and
has a delightful crunch in each spoonful. You can make the crumbs from any
leftover cakes, bread rolls, or from Prosecco Scones (page 280). When making
the crumbs needed for the dessert from leftover bread, make sure to add more
sugar to sweeten.

150g / 1¼ cups 2- to 3-day-old
 Prosecco Scones (page 280),
 white loaf bread, or cake, diced
 into 2cm / ¾-inch cubes

2 tablespoons salted butter,
 room temperature

1 tablespoon sugar

½ teaspoon ground cinnamon

Apple Mash (recipe follows)

My Mother's Whipped Cream
 (page 125), for serving

Preheat the oven to 200°C / 400°F.

Spread the cake cubes in an even layer on a rimmed baking sheet. Dry in
the oven for 5 to 6 minutes. Reduce the heat to 100°C / 210°F and continue to
dry for another 10 to 15 minutes. Turn the oven off, open the door slightly, and
let the cubes cool completely. Whizz the cubes in a food processor until you
have superfine crumbs.

Heat a large frying pan over medium. Combine the butter, sugar, and cinnamon in the pan, then add the cake crumbs. (If you used plain white bread, you may want to add more sugar to taste.) Cook, stirring constantly, until the crumbs are dark golden, 6 to 8 minutes. You can use them now, or you can let them cool completely and store in an airtight jar for up to 2 weeks.

In 6 individual dessert cups or ramekins, place 1 tablespoon of toasted cake crumbs, 2 tablespoons of apple mash, and 2 tablespoons of whipped cream. Repeat the layering process once more. Serve immediately.

APPLE MASH

Serves 6

Traditionally served as part of the *Tilslørte Bondepiker* dessert, this is just as lovely warm over porridge or as a topping for pancakes. *Eple Mos*, as we call it in Norway, can be made in advance and stored in an airtight container in the refrigerator for 1 to 2 weeks.

100ml / ⅓ cup plus 1 tablespoon water	6 Granny Smith apples, peeled, cored, and chopped	1 teaspoon fresh lemon juice
50g / ¼ cup sugar		

In a medium saucepan set over medium-low heat, combine the water and sugar, and heat, stirring, until the sugar is dissolved, 1 to 2 minutes. Add the apples and lemon juice. Bring to a boil, then reduce the heat to medium-low, cover the pan, and let simmer, stirring occasionally, until the apples are completely soft, 18 to 22 minutes. Let cool.

MY GRANDMOTHER'S NO-BAKE
CHOCOLATE BISCUIT SLICE

Serves 8 to 10

This no-bake chocolate cake is from my grandmother's repertoire and is great to have on hand for those impromptu dinner parties with friends that simply call for a slice of decadence to round off a lovely meal. One can't go wrong with chocolate, sweetened with candied cherries and orange peel. It keeps well in the fridge for up to four days, so it can easily be made in advance. Cut thick slices and serve chilled on individual plates with a strong cup of black coffee, just like my grandmother did.

---

2 tablespoons double cream / heavy cream

200g / 7 ounces dark chocolate, broken into pieces

150g / 5 ounces coconut oil

100g / ½ cup sugar

2 medium eggs

1 tablespoon vanilla paste

1½ tablespoons candied orange and lemon peel

1 tablespoon chopped glacé cherries, plus 4 halved cherries for garnish

9 Marie or digestive biscuits (graham crackers will also work)

In a small saucepan set over medium-low heat, heat the cream for 1 minute. Reduce the heat to low, add the chocolate and coconut oil, and stir until melted. Remove from the heat and let cool until the mixture is lukewarm.

In a medium bowl, beat together the sugar, eggs, and vanilla paste until creamy, 12 to 13 minutes. (Alternatively, beat using a hand mixer for about 3 minutes.) Gently fold in the chocolate mixture, then fold in the mixed peel and cherries.

Line a small rectangular 9 × 24-centimeter / 3½ × 9½-inch baking dish, or a standard loaf pan, with parchment paper, overlapping the edges. Pour in a quarter of the chocolate mixture. Place 3 biscuits over the chocolate layer, then repeat twice more with another layer of chocolate and biscuits to make 3 layers, ending with a layer of chocolate. Arrange the cherry halves in a row across the top. Refrigerate for 2 to 3 hours before serving.

To serve, cut into 1- to 2-centimeter / ½-inch slices, using a sharp knife.

CARAMEL POPCORN

Serves 4 to 6

For my birthday, my mother would let me have any dessert I wanted. Giddy with excitement, I'd urge her to make a batch of golden popcorn. And since I requested the same thing every year, it became a tradition. She'd make it in huge quantities the morning of my big day, to the delight of all my friends and family who came over to celebrate. We'd all relish in scoffing down mouthfuls of this crunchy, salty, and sweet treat. Nowadays, I love serving it with a sparkling wine after dinner.

POPCORN

3 tablespoons olive oil

4 tablespoons popcorn kernels

Melted butter, for parchment

CARAMEL SAUCE

175g / ¾ cup packed light brown sugar

100ml / ⅓ cup plus 1 tablespoon light golden syrup (available at Amazon.com)

125g / ⅔ cup salted butter, cubed

1 teaspoon vanilla paste

1 teaspoon baking powder

Sea salt

In a large saucepan set over medium heat, heat the oil. Add the kernels and cover. The kernels will begin to pop once they get hot enough. When the popping sound dies out, remove the pan from the heat and pour the popcorn into a large bowl. (You can also use a standard-size, unflavored popcorn packet.)

Preheat the oven to 100°C / 210°F. Line 1 large or 2 small rimmed baking sheets with lightly buttered parchment paper.

MAKE THE CARAMEL SAUCE: In a medium saucepan set over low heat, combine the sugar and syrup. Let cook, occasionally swirling gently but not stirring, until the sugar has dissolved, 3 to 5 minutes. Add the butter and swirl the pan to combine well until the butter melts, 2 to 3 minutes. Remove the pan from the heat, add the vanilla paste and baking powder, and stir well. Working quickly, pour the warm caramel sauce over the popcorn in the bowl. Using a flexible spatula, make sure that all of the popcorn is generously coated with the caramel. Spread the popcorn out onto the prepared baking sheets.

Bake, stirring the popcorn every 10 minutes, until crunchy, about 1 hour.

Before serving, sprinkle with sea salt. Enjoy warm or room temperature.

RHUBARB LEMONADE

Makes 1⅔L / 6½ cups

Refreshing on a warm spring day, this rhubarb lemonade makes a lovely non-alcoholic option for a pre-dinner drink, simply mixed with still or sparkling water. Every now and then, for special occasions, I mix it with chilled champagne and decorate the glasses with a sprinkle of "frost" by rubbing lemon juice on the rims before dipping the glasses in sugar. Think rhubarb Bellini. My mother makes this lemonade as long as rhubarb is in season, which can last from spring well into the early autumn months. Freeze the lemonade for a special midwinter drink.

1½L / 6⅓ cups water	1 vanilla bean	2 lemons, sliced
500g / 2½ cups sugar	1kg / 2.2 pounds rhubarb, cut into 2cm / ¾-inch pieces	Juice of 1 lemon

In a large saucepan set over high heat, bring the water and sugar to a boil. Split the vanilla bean in half lengthwise and use the back of a knife to scrape the seeds into the pan of sugar water. Add the bean to the pan.

In a large bowl, combine the rhubarb, lemon slices, and lemon juice. Pour the hot sugar-water mixture over the rhubarb. Let cool. Cover and leave in a cool place or refrigerator for 3 days. Give the lemonade a quick stir each day. On the third day, strain the lemonade through a fine-mesh sieve or cheesecloth.

The lemonade will keep in an airtight container in the refrigerator for up to 7 days.

To serve, mix 1 part lemonade with 1 part water, or as desired to achieve the right strength.

OPTIONAL: Sterilize bottles (see Tip, page 69) large enough to hold the lemonade and pour in the strained lemonade.

BRANDY HOT CHOCOLATE
WITH CARDAMOM

Makes 500ml / 2 cups

Having grown up with milk-based hot chocolate simmering away on the stove throughout the colder months of the year, I can't think of anything more delicious for a warm drink. We didn't drink much tea in my childhood home, so this was our go-to treat. While I've come to adore the thick, silky-smooth hot chocolate served in Italian bars—especially the one prepared by the skillful hands at Marchesi in Milan—I reserve it for when I'm traveling so the novelty won't wear off. As I settled into my cottage in England, I found myself yearning for my mother's hot chocolate one chilly afternoon, so I made a cup. Sipping it while reading a book in a chair next to my drinks tray, I reached for a bottle of brandy to bring an extra touch of flavor and warmth to this childhood favorite. An adult hot chocolate best enjoyed piping hot in small cups, it's a great nightcap after a meal with friends. For a nonalcoholic alternative, simply omit the brandy.

500ml / 2 cups plus 2 tablespoons whole milk

2 to 3 tablespoons My Mother's Chocolate Sauce (page 240)

¼ teaspoon ground cardamom

¼ teaspoon ground cinnamon

¼ teaspoon sea salt

2 to 3 tablespoons brandy (to taste)

In a medium saucepan set over low heat, combine the milk, chocolate sauce, cardamom, cinnamon, and salt. Bring to a gentle simmer, stirring gently until the chocolate sauce is dissolved and all the spices are well combined, 2 to 3 minutes. Add the brandy, stir well, and serve while hot.

summer

M Y PARENTS HOSTED MANY DINNER PARTIES when I was growing up, seating friends, family, and strangers around our dining room table frequently. I'd peek through the railings on the second floor, looking at who came through the front door in the evenings, watching coats and hats being hung in the mirrored closet in the hallway, and I would beam with excitement. Too worked up to sleep, I listened to their laughter rising up from below. Knowing I'd be called upon to introduce myself, my stomach would be filled with dancing butterflies as soon as I heard the cars drive up to our home.

My father was famous for calling home late in the afternoons to let my mother know he would be bringing guests for dinner that evening. With only hours to prepare, my mother wouldn't hesitate. She knew my father well, and when he called, the information was never phrased as a question; it was a statement. "I'm bringing five businessmen from France home for supper tonight," he'd say. "It's so much nicer to bring them for a home-cooked meal than to eat at a restaurant in town," he'd add before hanging up. My mother may have sighed with perhaps a smidge of despair as she stood there on the other end of the line with a toddler on her hip and another one running around causing mischief, knowing she had washing on the line. But she was resourceful and loved hosting.

Being of a generation that was used to cooking from their well-stocked pantry, rather than going out shopping for ingredients for a specific dish, she was, and still is, an incredible cook. To this day I'm in deep admiration and awe for how elegantly she whizzed together meals fit for a king in no time. My father was always pleased, and kissed her proudly after the guests returned to their hotel after dinner, leaving piles of plates and empty glasses behind. "I'm one lucky man," he'd tell her with warmth in his voice. I imagine my father, as someone who doesn't cook, had little understanding of exactly how much had gone into the meal he and his guests had just enjoyed with such gusto. My mother, still dressed in her serving apron, would turn toward him, smile, and perhaps cheekily think to herself, *ignorance is truly bliss.*

"It's all in the way it's served," she'd tell me when I asked how she managed to always have something delicious appear on the table as the cars arrived with my dad and a trail of businessmen. "If something is served on a nice tray, with thought to detail, no matter how simple it is, no one will ever raise an eyebrow. And make sure to give your guests something to drink as soon as they walk through the door," she'd add. Hosting is truly a skill, and I still have much to learn from the women in my family and their ability to resourcefully cook up a feast from what they have in their pantry. It seems like a dying skill, one that I eagerly incorporate into the way I cook.

ELDERFLOWERS BLOSSOMED AND SCENTED the countryside with the sweet perfume of summer during the months of May and June in my new cottage. Wearing knee-length dresses, I biked down narrow country paths and green lanes in search of edible flowers and plants to fill my basket. In a way, I felt as though I was becoming my mother.

A few years earlier, I dressed in high heels, skinny black trousers, and a chic little jacket, boarding airplanes with a perfectly packed carry-on, bound for New York, Paris, or Madrid. Eating out was a treasured pastime, one I took great pleasure in and still do. Yet in this move to the countryside—keeping only one pair of incredibly pointy handmade Italian leather heels to make room for my ever-growing collection of wellies—were tangible signs that something was shifting. There was an inner seasonal change. There was a return to the principles, values, and familiar rhythms of my youth, and there was a change in the way I dressed, reaching for skirts and dresses like my mother.

A heat wave swept through the countryside my first summer in the cottage, and people talked about nothing else when I passed them on my way to the greengrocer at the top of the hill. "It's positively tropical!" they'd exclaim. I smiled as I popped in for afternoon tea at my local antiques shop to see Russel, a trusted antiques dealer who partially furnished my cottage with his exciting finds. "Anything new in?" I'd ask as soon as he emerged from the storage room in the back upon hearing the doorbell ring. Antlers, old French flour sacks, worn rugs, and little stools—I never left our weekly afternoon tea empty-handed.

My circle of friends in my new town steadily expanded. People tipped their hats and waved hello as I passed by on my daily walks through town to pick up the newspaper and a bottle of milk. Just as a house doesn't become a home overnight, neither does a new town. You need to allow time for it to introduce itself to you. Gently stepping on its cobblestone streets, sipping tea in its tearooms, and uttering polite phrases about the weather when meeting new people help pave the way.

I'd met Russel during one of my first weeks in town. His well-stocked and ever-so-enticing antiques store just a stone's throw away from the cottage was an inviting warm nook to duck into on my way to the post office during winter. By spring, I had bought too many of his antiques not to be invited in for tea, and by summer I found myself completely spellbound listening to his buying adventures from his monthly travels to markets across England and abroad, in particular Istanbul. I loved his stories of navigating his way through the many narrow back lanes and souks, passing spice and date vendors with his arms firmly wrapped around his latest carpet purchase draped over his shoulders. His colorful travel stories filled my imagination and gave me just enough of the world beyond the shire to not miss it too much.

I slept with the windows open that warm summer, listening to the quiet sounds of the countryside, familiarizing myself with the songs of the English birds and the sound of the nearby trees rattling in the warm summer breeze. *Was this really me?* I wondered as Mr. Whiskey lay sprawled out next to my bed, enjoying the cool night breeze. There I was in a small cottage with a white picket fence, a garden, and a dog, dressed in an apron more often than a cocktail dress. Was this the new me? Or perhaps the me I'd always been, but I'd been running too fast to hear my own heartbeat? I discovered a newfound peace, and a slower way of life, yet perhaps I also discovered how little I knew myself.

"Is this me?" I asked my mother when we spoke on the phone next. I could hear her comforting smile on the other end.

"Only you can tell," she answered wisely, before asking me how I felt when I was in my cottage, or wandering through town, walking my dog, or cooking in my little cottage kitchen. "I feel at home," I answered before I even had time to properly think about her questions. "It's like I'm discovering myself for the very first time," I said, sinking into my grandmother's chair by the window. "I feel like I'm beginning to own myself rather than trying to please others. I feel like I've perhaps been like this all along, yet didn't know when to hop off the fast-moving and exciting carousel that simply keeps spinning until you chose to hop off and seek another ride."

I could hear her nodding on the other end. "Then this is you," she said calmly. "This is the you that you were as a child, yet it's also the woman you've become, and not a single ride in between has been in vain. Not a single choice, journey, or experience has been in vain; you simply happened to stop and reexamine where you were headed. You paused long enough to hear your own heartbeat," she continued, "and that is where magic begins."

I sighed with a happy smile on my face upon hearing those words. Happy and grateful, I sank farther down in my grandmother's chair by the window. Perhaps this wasn't so wrong after all; perhaps this was exactly where I was supposed to be at exactly the right time.

"Did you receive my letter?" my mother asked before we hung up. I replied that I did. "Go on a wander and fill your basket with blooming elderflowers," she suggested, "and make my elderflower pancakes. I think you'll love them," she added.

"I love you," I said as I picked up her letter from the small table in the kitchen corner, with her handwritten recipe carefully scribbled down on the back. "I love you too," she replied.

STARTERS AND SIDES

Artichokes with My Mother's
Creamy Lemon Butter Sauce

Elderflower Fritters

Strawberry and Ricotta Crostini

Tomato Tarte Tatin with Burrata

Spinach and Goat Cheese Frittata

Fried Zucchini Blossoms
with Anchovy Mayonnaise

Tomato, Olive, and Mozzarella
Baked Peppers

Norwegian Open-Faced Shrimp
and Dill Sandwich

MAINS

Port Baked Figs and
Camembert Pizza

Summer Panzanella

My Mother's Sour Cream
Porridge

Whole Baked Salmon with
Ginger and Basil

Spicy Summer Fish Stew

Norwegian Yellow Pea Soup
with Thyme

My Mother's Garden Soup

DESSERTS

Almond Rice Cream Pudding
with Raspberry Sauce

Red Currants and Strawberries
with White Caramel Sauce

Elderflower Norwegian Pancakes

Blackcurrant Porridge
with Pearl Barley

Limoncello Panna Cotta
with Passion Fruit

DRINKS AND JAMS

Blackcurrant and
Cinnamon Toddy

My Mother's Raw Elderflower
Cordial

Rosewater and Strawberry Jam

ARTICHOKES WITH MY MOTHER'S CREAMY LEMON BUTTER SAUCE

Serves 4

I fell head over heels in love with this spiky, green-blue-purple vegetable when I studied in Milan in my early twenties, but my love for artichokes was sealed when I ate my way through Rome during my time studying Caravaggio ten years later. Deep-fried, raw, pickled, or steamed, I haven't met an artichoke I haven't liked. When prepared in this simple way, all I do is dip each leaf in my mother's lemony butter sauce. After each bite there's a gentle and slowly emerging aftertaste of licorice that has me return again and again to this simple dish. Serve it with a dry white wine or a bit of bubbles, and you have a starter that's perfect for any summer party.

---

4 globe artichokes

My Mother's Creamy Lemon Butter Sauce (recipe follows), for serving

---

Using kitchen shears, cut the thorny tips off the petals on the artichokes. Pull and remove the small leaves from the base. Using a sharp paring knife, slice off the top of the artichoke, about 5 centimeters / 2 inches from the crown. Place the artichokes in a large saucepan with enough water to cover them completely. Cover and set the pan over medium heat. Bring the water to a simmer and cook until the artichokes are tender when tested with a fork, 18 to 25 minutes. Using a slotted spoon, transfer the artichokes to a wire rack to drain for a couple of minutes.

To serve, tear off a leaf, dip it into the butter sauce, and use your teeth to scrape off the flesh of the artichoke. Remember to provide an extra plate for the discarded leaves.

MY MOTHER'S CREAMY LEMON BUTTER SAUCE

Makes 200ml / scant 1 cup

100ml / ⅓ cup plus 1 tablespoon double cream / heavy cream

125g / ⅓ cup plus 1 tablespoon cold salted butter, cubed

½ teaspoon fresh lemon juice

¼ teaspoon sea salt

½ teaspoon finely chopped fresh chives

In a medium saucepan set over medium heat, bring the cream to a boil. Remove the pan from the heat and whisk in the butter a few pieces at a time. The butter should be mixed constantly, rather than being left to melt, in order to achieve the right color and taste. Whisk until the sauce thickens, placing it back on the heat and adding more butter if necessary. Whisk in the lemon juice, and season with the salt and chives. Serve warm from a bowl.

ELDERFLOWER FRITTERS

Makes 15 fritters

When warming winds caress the garden, it's so tempting to carry out the dining room table, dress it up, and throw an impromptu al fresco dinner party. In June, when light summer dresses and ballet flats become my uniform, fritters are often on the menu. In particular, elderflower fritters, with a wee sprinkle of both confectioners' sugar and sea salt. Best served right out of the frying pan with a sparkling wine, they're a lovely, gently flavored snack to whet the appetite with.

140g / 1 cup all-purpose flour

Pinch of sea salt, plus more
 for serving

1 medium egg

180ml / ¾ cup prosecco

15 elderflower heads

1½L / 6⅓ cups vegetable oil

1 to 2 bread crumbs, to test the oil

Icing sugar / confectioners' sugar,
 for serving

Sift the flour into a medium bowl and add the salt and egg. Slowly pour in the prosecco and mix well until a nice batter forms. Cover and let the batter rest for 30 minutes on the counter.

Rinse the elderflower heads in cold water. Shake off any excess water and let them dry on a kitchen towel.

In a large saucepan set over medium-high heat, heat the oil to 180°C / 350°F. Test the oil with a bread crumb or two to see if it's hot enough; the oil should bubble around the bread immediately upon dropping it in. Using tongs, pick up each flower head, dip it generously in the batter, and submerge the flower head in the hot oil for a few seconds, until it has a deep golden color. Using a slotted spoon, transfer fried flowers to a wire rack and let drain. Repeat with the remaining flower heads.

Serve immediately with a generous sprinkle of confectioners' sugar.

STRAWBERRY AND RICOTTA CROSTINI

Serves 4 to 6

This fresh little bite is wonderful on hot summer days when you gather friends and family in the garden for pre-dinner drinks. Quick to make and full of summer, it's a winner served with bubbles or a blushing rosé. Arrange on a large tray with plenty for all. The quality of the strawberries is imperative, as is the freshness of the mint and ricotta cheese. In simple dishes, every little ingredient matters, and together they create the best flavor.

10 baguette slices, sliced on an angle

125g / 1 cup fresh ricotta

125g / 2 cups fresh strawberries, quartered

Fresh mint, for garnish

Aceto Balsamico di Modena vinegar, or another quality balsamic vinegar

Salt and coarsely ground black pepper

Toast the baguette slices, then spread each slice with fresh ricotta. Divide the strawberries among the slices, and garnish with mint before carefully sprinkling 2 to 3 drops of the vinegar over each crostini. Sprinkle with salt and pepper.

TOMATO TARTE TATIN
WITH BURRATA

Serves 6 to 8

I discovered tarte tatin years ago when I lived in Annecy, France. During my childhood years, we would rent a summer house by the lake there, and I returned in my late teens to study French. In a small restaurant tucked away on a back street by the river, I had tarte tatin for the first time, and since then I've experimented with many different versions. I usually make dessert variations; however, when tomatoes are in season, I make this savory version. It's a great picnic lunch, as well as a starter. I enjoy it with torn burrata cheese on top, but that's an optional addition. Serve warm with a dry white wine or a gentle red.

1 large red onion, halved and thinly sliced

1 teaspoon salted butter

3 tablespoons honey

1 teaspoon red wine vinegar

400g / 14 ounces cherry or grape tomatoes (yellow, red, orange), halved

½ cup green or black olives

1½ teaspoons finely chopped fresh thyme

Sea salt and coarsely ground black pepper

170g / 6 ounces puff pastry

125g / 4.4 ounces fresh burrata, torn into pieces (optional)

Olive oil, for drizzling

Fresh basil, torn, for garnish

Preheat the oven to 220°C / 425°F with racks set in the middle and the bottom third.

In a large, ovenproof skillet set over low heat, cook the onions in the butter, stirring occasionally, until caramelized, 8 to 10 minutes. Transfer to a plate and set aside. Keep the skillet handy.

In a separate small skillet set over medium heat, bring the honey to a gentle simmer and cook, swirling the skillet occasionally (do not stir), until warmed through and slightly thickened, 5 to 6 minutes. Add the vinegar and cook, swirling the pan until combined, 2 to 3 minutes. Add the tomatoes, olives, thyme, salt, and pepper and toss to coat. Pour the tomato mixture into

recipe continues

the skillet that the onions were cooked in, arranging it into a heap in the middle as much as you can, so you will have room to tuck the pastry around everything. Pile the onions on top.

On a lightly floured work surface, roll out the puff pastry and cut a circular piece slightly larger than the skillet. Lay the pastry over the tomatoes and onions in the skillet and tuck any excess down under the vegetables.

Place the skillet in the middle of the oven and bake until cooked through, 27 to 30 minutes. If it browns too quickly, move it to the bottom rack. After removing the tart from the oven, let it cool for a few minutes before placing a large plate upside down on top of the skillet. Using oven mitts, press the plate down and quickly flip the skillet and the plate so the skillet is upside down and the tart dislodges onto the plate. Carefully remove the skillet.

Scatter the torn pieces of burrata on top of the tart, if desired. Serve warm, drizzled with olive oil and sprinkled with the basil and pepper.

SPINACH AND GOAT CHEESE FRITTATA

Serves 4 to 6

We had chickens on the farm I grew up on in Norway in a small coop next to the pond at the bottom of the garden, and one of my daily duties as a little girl was to collect the eggs. I'd carefully carry them through the garden and hand them to my mother. She'd make omelets, or boil the eggs and serve them cold on slices of bread with herring fillets and sour cream, or use them for quiches and frittatas. Spinach and goat cheese, which I've used in this frittata, make a lovely match, but other cheeses work well too. My friend Heather adds potatoes and asparagus to hers, which makes it into a wonderfully fulfilling meal. A frittata is a blank canvas to which you can add any seasonal produce you'd like. Serve warm or at room temperature with in-season salad leaves as garnish and a side of freshly baked bread.

---

1 tablespoon salted butter, plus more for greasing

1 teaspoon olive oil

2 shallots, finely chopped

1 garlic clove, finely chopped

130g / 10 cups fresh baby spinach, washed well and drained

100g / 1 cup chopped slab pancetta

8 medium eggs

Sea salt and coarsely ground black pepper

80ml / 1/3 cup double cream / heavy cream

70g / 1/4 cup goat cheese, crumbled

Preheat the oven to 180°C / 350°F. Butter a deep 26-centimeter / 10-inch round pie dish or skillet.

In a large, ovenproof skillet set over medium heat, melt the butter and oil. Add the shallots and garlic and cook, stirring, until soft, 3 to 4 minutes. Add the spinach and cook, stirring, until slightly wilted, 2 to 3 minutes.

In a small skillet set over medium heat, fry the pancetta until cooked through and golden, 2 to 3 minutes.

In a large bowl, whisk the eggs, season with salt and pepper, and stir in the cream. Pour the egg mixture into the prepared pie dish or skillet. Sprinkle the spinach mixture, pancetta, and goat cheese over the egg mixture. Bake until puffed up and cooked through, 13 to 15 minutes.

FRIED ZUCCHINI BLOSSOMS
WITH ANCHOVY MAYONNAISE

Serves 6

One early summer's day, I traveled to Tuscany to attend a dear friend's wedding. My friend Peter and I enjoyed a few days in a villa in the mountains before meeting up with the rest of the party. During our stay, we met the villa's in-house chef, Alexis Delaney, who one morning took us zucchini blossom picking in the large kitchen garden. She deep-fried the blossoms to crispy perfection as part of a farewell brunch, and kindly shared her recipe with me. This is a simple dish, and the prosecco truly makes a difference in the batter, making it fluffy and light, while the anchovy mayonnaise cuts through with its fresh and salty flavors. I've enjoyed re-creating this wonderful dish over and over again in my English cottage kitchen.

---

24 courgette / zucchini blossoms, ideally with tiny zucchini attached

1½L / 6⅓ cups vegetable oil

40g / ⅓ cup all-purpose flour

30g / ¼ cup rice flour

160ml / ⅔ cup prosecco

Sea salt

Anchovy Mayonnaise (recipe follows), for serving

Gently wash the zucchini blossoms and baby zucchini in a bowl of water and place on a kitchen towel to dry.

Fill a large saucepan with the vegetable oil, but no higher than halfway or you run the risk of boiling over. Heat the oil until a deep-fry thermometer reads 180°C / 350°F. Line a plate with paper towels and set it next to the pot.

In a medium bowl, whisk together the flours and prosecco until just barely combined. Do not overmix. Working in batches of 4 or 5, dip the blossoms in the batter, coating them evenly. Lay the battered blossoms in the oil. Cook, flipping the blossoms once with a slotted spoon, until golden brown, 2 to 3 minutes. Transfer to the paper towel–lined plate to drain. Season liberally with sea salt and repeat with the remaining blossoms.

Enjoy as soon as they are cool enough to handle, with anchovy mayonnaise on the side for dipping.

ANCHOVY MAYONNAISE

Makes about 1 cup

---

1 egg yolk

1 tablespoon fresh lemon
   juice

180ml / ¾ cup vegetable oil

60ml / ¼ cup olive oil

1 garlic clove

4 anchovy fillets

Sea salt

In a small bowl, whisk together the egg yolk and lemon juice until light in color. Whisking constantly, very slowly, drop by drop, add the vegetable oil and then the olive oil.

In a mortar and pestle, pound the garlic and the anchovy fillets until smooth. Whisk the mixture into the mayonnaise, and let stand for 1 minute. Check the seasoning, adding a pinch of salt if needed.

TOMATO, OLIVE, AND MOZZARELLA BAKED PEPPERS

Serves 4

It always surprises me how flavorful peppers become when they're roasted. I usually turn up the heat slightly and put them up underneath the broiler to blacken the edges right before serving, and they turn very sweet as a result. Roasted peppers don't hold their shape very well, so they are best enjoyed straight out of the oven. Serve with some sourdough bread on the side to mop up the juices.

---

2 red bell peppers, halved lengthwise and seeded (leave the stems on)

Olive oil, for drizzling

50g / 1.7 ounces cherry tomatoes on the vine, halved

50g / 1.7 ounces black pitted olives

125g / 4½ ounces small mozzarella balls

Sea salt and freshly ground black pepper

1 tablespoon Aceto Balsamico di Modena vinegar (optional), for drizzling

2 tablespoons roughly chopped fresh basil, for garnish

Preheat the oven to 180°C / 350°F.

Place the peppers on a medium baking sheet, skin-side down, and drizzle with the olive oil. Roast until softened, 12 to 15 minutes. Remove the peppers from the oven. Keep the oven on.

Divide the tomatoes, olives, and mozzarella among the 4 pepper halves. Drizzle with olive oil and season with salt and pepper. Pop back in the oven to roast until cooked through and the cheese is melted, 10 to 12 minutes. If you like, increase the heat to broil and char briefly before serving, 1 to 2 minutes.

Put the peppers on 4 serving plates. Drizzle with the vinegar, if desired, and garnish with the basil. Serve hot.

NORWEGIAN OPEN-FACED SHRIMP AND DILL SANDWICH

Serves 2

On warm summer days, you'll find us Norwegians queuing up along the piers as the boats come in with freshly caught Atlantic shrimp. Cooking shrimp is ultimately a social event where everyone gets involved, peeling shrimp and arranging them on thick slices of generously buttered white country loaf, such as my No-Knead Country Loaf (page 32). This is a simple dish full of soothing salty flavors and textures, but it's also a celebration, as little says summer more than tucking into a homemade shrimp sandwich with friends and family around a long table set in the garden.

---

2 slices sourdough bread

1 tablespoon salted butter

2 tablespoons high-quality mayonnaise

250g / 8.8 ounces cooked Arctic prawns, shell on

Juice of ¼ lemon

2 fresh dill sprigs, for garnish

1 teaspoon coarsely ground black pepper, for garnish

Arrange the bread on individual serving plates and coat each slice with butter. Spread 1 tablespoon of mayonnaise on each slice. Peel the prawns and divide them between the 2 slices. Squeeze lemon juice over the top and garnish with dill and pepper. Serve immediately.

PORT BAKED FIGS
AND CAMEMBERT PIZZA

Makes 2 pizzas

When I lived in Rome, I ventured often to the Amalfi coast and to Napoli, where my passion for pizza was deepened. There are so many types of pizza, but the ones made in Napoli are my favorite, with their thin crusts and their wonderful attention to detail and the quality of the ingredients. I don't have a pizza oven, and I can't claim that mine really live up to the ones in Napoli, but I've included two of my go-to pizza recipes here—this one, which I make often during summer, and the Taleggio and Potato Pizza on page 97.

Pizza Dough (page 98)

8 ripe fresh figs, cut into bite-size pieces

1 teaspoon salted butter

3 tablespoons red port

40g / ¼ cup packed light brown sugar

Zest and juice of ½ unwaxed orange

250g / 9 ounces Camembert, roughly chopped

150g / 5 ounces goat cheese, roughly chopped

2 to 4 slices prosciutto, roughly torn

Sea salt and coarsely ground black pepper

Olive oil, for drizzling

Rocket / arugula, for garnish

1 tablespoon roughly torn fresh basil, for garnish

Bake the pizza dough according to the recipe directions.

Preheat the oven to 200°C / 400°F with a rack set in the middle.

Place the fig pieces in a small, deep baking dish. Add the butter, port, sugar, orange zest and juice and combine well. Put the dish on the middle rack of the oven and bake until the figs are tender, about 10 minutes. Drain, reserving the liquid in the bottom of the dish (see Tip).

Arrange the figs, Camembert, goat cheese, and prosciutto on the pizza crusts. Season with salt and pepper, and drizzle with olive oil. Transfer to the oven and bake until the cheese is golden and melted, 6 to 9 minutes.

Serve warm, sprinkled with a handful of arugula and basil.

TIP: Make an additional topping by simmering the reserved sauce from baking the figs until reduced by half. Drizzle over the pizza before serving.

SUMMER PANZANELLA

Serves 4

This version of the traditional Tuscan bread salad called *panzanella* is a staple in my cottage kitchen during the summer months. It's a comforting dish with lots of flavor and texture. That said, the quality of the ingredients is key, so be sure to select the finest you can find. There are many variations of this simple dish, but I prefer mine as paired down as possible, adding just a little bit of artichoke heart to the basic tomato, onion, and bread mixture. Serve at room temperature with a chilled dry white wine.

---

100 to 150g / 3 to 5 ounces stale artisan bread, such as a good sourdough, No-Knead Country Loaf (page 32), or Rosemary Breadsticks (page 92), torn into bite-size pieces

200ml / ¾ cup plus 1 tablespoon water

2 teaspoons red wine vinegar

350g / 12 ounces heirloom or cherry tomatoes

100 to 150g / ⅔ cup marinated artichoke hearts, drained and halved

1 red onion, sliced

3 to 4 tablespoons roughly chopped fresh basil

2 to 4 tablespoons olive oil

Sea salt and coarsely ground black pepper

In a large bowl, soak the bread pieces in the water and vinegar until soft but not soggy, 15 to 20 minutes.

Roughly cut the tomatoes into bite-size pieces if using heirloom or in half if using cherry. Put the chopped tomatoes into a large bowl and add the artichokes, onion, and basil. Drain and squeeze the bread, then add it to the tomato mixture. Pour in the olive oil, and season to taste with salt and pepper. Cover and let sit at room temperature for 10 to 15 minutes before serving.

MY MOTHER'S SOUR CREAM PORRIDGE

Serves 4 to 6

If there's one dish that stands out from my childhood, it's this porridge. Silky and smooth, savory yet sweet, it's the epitome of comfort food. All tucked up in warm blankets with a cold, when no food was tempting, my request was always the same. I would lie in my bed upstairs and listen to the rhythmic sound of my mother stirring the fresh sour cream into the warm milk, and the soothing, gentle aroma of warm porridge would fill our house. Traditionally it's served with buttered Norwegian flatbread and salt-cured meat on the side. In my family this would typically mean thinly cut slices of *fenalår*, salt-cured leg of mutton, though thin slices of Iberico ham are also delicious. But more often than not, I simply sprinkle mine with sugar and cinnamon and toss in a knob of butter.

300ml / 1¼ cups sour cream

1L / 4¼ cups whole milk

160g / 1¼ cups all-purpose flour

1 teaspoon sea salt

Sugar, for serving

Ground cinnamon, for serving

Salted butter, for serving

Norwegian flatbread (very crisp thin sheets of bread), buttered, for serving (optional)

Salt-cured meat, such as *fenalår*, Iberico ham, or prosciutto, for serving (optional)

In a large saucepan set over medium heat, place the sour cream. Add 2dl / 1 cup of the milk, followed by 3 tablespoons flour, and continue adding both, alternating wet and dry, while stirring continuously. Continue to stir until there are no lumps, then add the salt. Let cook, bubbling away while stirring, until the porridge is smooth, 8 to 10 minutes, over low heat.

Serve each bowl of porridge with a sprinkle of sugar and cinnamon and a small knob of butter. If desired, serve buttered flatbread and salt-cured meat on the side.

WHOLE BAKED SALMON
WITH GINGER AND BASIL

Serves 6 to 8

Whole baked salmon is summer to me. My mother would make it often when I was growing up, to the delight of the whole family. She'd stuff the inside of the fish with dill and lemon slices, and serve it with her creamy, irresistible butter sauce. One summer's day when a friend of mine came to an early supper in my cottage garden, I wanted to re-create this Norwegian classic. But as I began stuffing the fish with lemon slices, I discovered I didn't have much dill, so I went for basil I had growing in my garden, and included fresh ginger to add a bit of zing. I've never been very good at following a recipe, and I'm always adding new things and changing it up, which I hope you'll do too as you cook from this book and make the recipes your own. My friend and I enjoyed a lovely meal as the sun set that evening, and I've continued making this version of the dish ever since. It's a must to serve it with the Cucumber Salad (recipe follows), boiled potatoes, and My Mother's Creamy Lemon Butter Sauce (page 145); steamed carrots and sweet pea sides are optional.

Sea salt and coarsely ground black pepper

600 to 800g / 1½ to 2 pounds whole wild salmon, gutted

2 lemons, sliced

5 to 7 centimeters / 2 to 3 inches fresh ginger, peeled and sliced

5 fresh basil sprigs

Two batches My Mother's Creamy Lemon Butter Sauce (page 145), for serving

Cucumber Salad (recipe follows), for serving

Boiled potatoes, for serving

Preheat the oven to 200°C / 400°F with an oven rack set in the middle. Line a large rimmed baking sheet with aluminum foil. The sheet should be large enough to fit the fish, and the foil should be large enough to wrap over the fish.

Generously sprinkle salt and pepper on the foil before placing the fish on top. Layer the lemon slices inside the fish, then insert the ginger slices and basil. Generously season the inside and the top with salt and pepper before wrapping the foil around the fish, covering it completely. Fold and seal the corners like a parcel.

Place the baking sheet in the oven and bake for 25 to 30 minutes. Open the foil, exposing the fish completely, and bake until cooked through, 5 to 8 minutes more.

Serve warm with My Mother's Creamy Lemon Butter Sauce and a side of cucumber salad and boiled potatoes.

TIP: Ask your local fishmonger to source a whole wild salmon for you. If you can't get one, a farmed whole salmon or trout will suffice. Ask the fishmonger to keep the whole fish intact, but to gut and rinse it for you.

CUCUMBER SALAD

Serves 6 to 8

1½ (450g / 15 ounces) English cucumbers, chilled and sliced paper thin	1 tablespoon sugar, or to taste ½ teaspoon sea salt	¼ teaspoon coarsely ground black pepper Juice of ½ lemon

Place the sliced cucumber in a medium bowl. Sprinkle the sugar, salt, pepper, and lemon juice over the cucumber, and lightly toss together. This salad is best served immediately; otherwise the cucumber will begin to get soggy.

SPICY SUMMER FISH STEW

Serves 4 to 6

My first summer at the cottage, I don't think a week went by without some form of fish appearing on my dinner table. I was never a fish-loving child, yet after spending time in Tokyo from seventeen to eighteen, I came to adore sushi, and thus a love for fish was born. This soup has a deep and spicy aroma that makes it a delicious, warming meal. During cool summer days in my English town, I return to my kitchen and cook up this rich stew to stay warm. Make sure to have buttered bread on hand, such as my Rosemary Breadsticks (page 92) or No-Knead Country Loaf (page 32), to soak up the juices from the stew.

½ teaspoon coriander seeds, coarsely crushed

1 teaspoon fennel seeds, coarsely crushed

1 whole star anise, coarsely crushed

1 tablespoon salted butter

2 tablespoons olive oil

1 medium yellow onion, chopped

2 celery stalks, finely chopped

2 garlic cloves, chopped

2 tablespoons tomato puree

Pinch of crushed red pepper flakes

1 tablespoon finely chopped fresh coriander / cilantro

900ml / 3¾ cups hot fish stock

Pinch of saffron

600g / 1.4 pounds whole spring potatoes, scrubbed

Sea salt

500g / 1 pound cod, salmon, monkfish, or other firm white fish (a combination is best), chopped

100g / 3½ ounces whole shrimp, shell on

In a large saucepan set over medium heat, toast the coriander, fennel, and anise, constantly stirring or shaking the pan to prevent burning, until fragrant, 30 seconds. Set the seeds aside in a bowl.

In the same pan set over medium heat, heat the butter and olive oil. Add the onions, celery, and garlic and cook, stirring, until soft, 10 to 15 minutes. Stir in the tomato puree, red pepper flakes, cilantro, and the toasted seeds.

In another medium saucepan set over medium heat, bring the fish stock to a boil. Stir in the saffron. Pour the stock into the onion and tomato mixture.

In a separate medium saucepan set over high heat, boil the whole potatoes in salted water until tender, 16 to 19 minutes. Drain, allow to cool slightly, then cut each potato into 4 pieces, and add them to the stew. Add the fish and shrimp and cook, stirring occasionally, until cooked through, 2 to 3 minutes.

NORWEGIAN YELLOW PEA SOUP
WITH THYME

Serves 6 to 8

This is a hearty traditional Norwegian soup that my mother makes on a regular basis, and despite the name it is not vegetarian—its flavor comes from ham cooked on the bone. It's a quiet soup that has a soothing and comforting aroma. It takes a bit of forethought, as the dried peas cannot be substituted with fresh, and you need to soak the peas overnight. But once the peas have been left to soak, a single pot heating on the stovetop does the rest. After it has lent its flavor and marrow to the soup, cut the ham into small pieces and add it to the soup, or cut it into thin slices to use as sandwich meat for lunch the next day.

500g / 2⅔ cups dried whole yellow peas

1 to 2 teaspoons salted butter

2 celery stalks, finely chopped

1 yellow onion, finely chopped

2 carrots, chopped

1 leek, halved lengthwise, cleaned well, and finely sliced

1 ham hock on the bone (¼kg / 3 pounds), skinless

1.7L / scant 7¼ cups water, plus more for soaking peas

2 fresh bay leaves

3 to 4 fresh thyme sprigs

1 fresh rosemary sprig

Sea salt and coarsely ground black pepper

Place the peas in a large bowl, cover with water, and leave to soak overnight.

When the peas are done soaking, in a large saucepan set over medium heat, melt the butter. Add the celery, onion, carrots, and leek, and cook, stirring, until tender, 3 to 4 minutes. Add the ham hock and brown on all sides, 3 to 4 minutes.

Drain and discard the water from the peas and add the peas to the saucepan. Add the water, bay leaves, thyme, and rosemary. Bring to a boil, then reduce to a simmer and cook until the peas are soft, 65 to 70 minutes, removing and discarding any foam that gathers on the surface. Remove the pork and set aside. Season generously with salt and pepper. Before serving, remove and discard the bay leaves and thyme and rosemary sprigs.

Serve warm with a portion of shredded ham to garnish, if desired.

MY MOTHER'S GARDEN SOUP

Serves 4 to 6

Just as I crave hearty stews during winter, I crave rich vegetable soups during summer. My mother makes the most wonderful soups, and this is one that I ask her to make again and again. Filled to the brim with the cream of the crop from her garden, this dish nourishes and rejuvenates. It can easily be made in advance and kept warm on the stovetop until your dinner guests arrive, and is just as delicious the next day. Make sure you have some bread on hand to dip into the soup, and serve hot with a chilled rosé or a gentle red.

75g / ½ cup pearl barley

1 teaspoon sea salt, plus more for seasoning

150ml / ½ cup plus 2 tablespoons cold water, plus more if needed

2 tablespoons salted butter or olive oil

¼ fresh red chili pepper, seeded and finely chopped

1 garlic clove, finely chopped

1 celery stalk, thinly sliced

2 centimeters / ¾ inch fresh ginger, peeled and finely chopped

50g / 1½ ounces parsnip, finely chopped

350g / 12 ounces white cabbage, finely chopped

150g / 5 ounces swede / rutabaga, finely sliced then chopped

1 large carrot, halved lengthwise then finely sliced

100g / 3 ounces leek, cleaned well and finely sliced

1L / 4¼ cups chicken or vegetable stock

½ teaspoon finely chopped fresh thyme

¼ teaspoon fennel seeds

Coarsely ground black pepper

Tabasco sauce (optional)

Roughly chopped fresh coriander / cilantro, for garnish

Place the barley and salt in a medium saucepan and cover with the cold water. Bring to a boil over high heat. Reduce the heat to low, cover, and simmer until the barley is tender, adding more water to the pan if it becomes dry, 30 to 40 minutes. Drain and set the barley aside.

In a large saucepan set over medium-high heat, melt the butter. Add the chili, garlic, celery, ginger, parsnip, cabbage, rutabaga, carrot, and leek, and sauté, 4 to 6 minutes. Add the stock and barley, increase the heat to high, and bring to a boil. Cook for 1 minute before lowering the heat to medium-low. Simmer until the vegetables and barley are soft, 15 to 18 minutes. Add the thyme and fennel seeds, and season with salt and pepper to taste. Add the Tabasco to taste, if using. Serve hot in bowls, garnished with cilantro.

ALMOND RICE CREAM PUDDING WITH RASPBERRY SAUCE

Serves 4 to 6

I often have traditional Norwegian rice cream porridge for dinner, which always leaves me with leftovers, as my eyes are usually bigger than my stomach. And I love to take that excess and make this dead-easy dessert. Should you not have any leftover Norwegian Sweet Rice Cream Porridge (page 42), simply follow the recipe below. You can make the red sauce from most berries and fruit, but I prefer to use purple plums or raspberries for a sweet, deep red sauce. This dish is a simple crowd-pleaser that you can easily make in advance and keep cool in the fridge, ready to be served. Serve chilled with the raspberry sauce and a glass of port wine or hot black coffee.

RICE CREAM

300ml / 1¼ cups leftover Norwegian Sweet Rice Cream Porridge (page 42)

Or

200ml / ¾ cup plus 1 tablespoon water

100g / ½ cup risotto or Arborio rice

400ml / 1⅔ cups whole milk

Pinch of sea salt

ALMOND CREAM

400ml / 1⅔ cups double cream / heavy cream

1 tablespoon sugar

1 teaspoon vanilla paste

50g / ⅓ cup roughly chopped almonds

RASPBERRY SAUCE

300g / 2 cups fresh raspberries

400ml / 1⅔ cups water

100g / ½ cup sugar

2 tablespoons cornstarch

FOR THE RICE CREAM (if using leftover rice cream, skip this step): In a medium saucepan set over medium-high heat, bring the water and rice to a boil. Reduce the heat to low and simmer until the water has almost completely evaporated, 5 to 8 minutes. Give the rice a good stir and add the milk and pinch of salt. Increase the heat to medium and bring the mixture to a boil. Once boiling, reduce the heat to low, cover, and cook, stirring occasionally,

recipe continues

until soft, 55 to 60 minutes. Let cool completely, 1 to 2 hours, or overnight in the fridge.

FOR THE ALMOND CREAM: In a medium bowl, using an electric hand mixer, beat the cream, sugar, and vanilla paste until soft peaks form, 4 to 5 minutes. Using a flexible spatula, fold in the chopped almonds. Fold the almond cream mixture into the chilled rice.

FOR THE RASPBERRY SAUCE: In a medium saucepan set over medium heat, combine the raspberries and 300ml / 1⅓ cups water. Bring to a boil then reduce the heat to a simmer and cook until soft, 10 to 12 minutes. Strain the sauce through a fine-mesh sieve or cheesecloth if you wish to make the sauce clear and seed-free. Return the sauce to the pan set over medium heat and add the sugar. Bring the sauce to a boil and cook until the sugar is dissolved, 1 to 2 minutes.

Combine the cornstarch and remaining 100ml / ⅓ cup of water in a jar, tighten the lid, and shake until the cornstarch is dissolved and the mixture is smooth and lump-free. Pour the mixture into the sauce in a thin stream while stirring to combine. Cook until the sauce thickens, 1 to 2 minutes more.

Divide the pudding among individual serving bowls and pour the warm raspberry sauce on top.

RED CURRANTS AND STRAWBERRIES WITH WHITE CARAMEL SAUCE

Serves 4 to 6

As soon as the currants in our garden turn red, my mother makes this dessert. She traditionally omits the strawberries, but I adore the combination of sweet and sour, all embraced in a thick glossy layer of her famous white caramel sauce, which has roots in Finnish cuisine. It's fresh and ever so simple to make. Make sure you have access to seasonal, ripe berries; as with any simple dish, the secret is in the quality of ingredients. You can also make the sauce in advance and simply reheat it right before you assemble the dessert.

150g / ⅔ cup sugar

150ml / ½ cup plus 2 tablespoons
   double cream / heavy cream

350g / 2 cups strawberries,
   quartered

350g / 2⅓ cups red currants

In a small saucepan set over medium-low heat, combine the sugar and cream and bring the mixture to a simmer. Cook, stirring, until the sugar is dissolved, 3 to 5 minutes. Remove the pan from the heat and let cool until lukewarm.

Divide the berries among individual bowls and drizzle the white caramel sauce over them. Serve immediately.

ELDERFLOWER NORWEGIAN PANCAKES

Serves 4 to 6

My mother shared this recipe with me in a letter during my first summer in my cottage. It's a simple dessert, paired down so that the syrup made from the elderflower cordial can truly shine. I sometimes simply roll up a pancake sprinkled with sugar and dip it into the syrup for a little afternoon treat on a particularly warm summer's day. I'm not a big ice cream lover, but this dessert works really well topped off with vanilla ice cream. Serve warm with a sweet dessert wine like Vin Santo or Marsala or a cheeky glass of prosecco.

---

4 medium eggs

2 tablespoons sugar

Pinch of sea salt

600ml / 2½ cups whole milk (or water)

150ml / ½ cup plus 2 tablespoons My Mother's Raw Elderflower Cordial (page 184), or a good-quality store-bought elderflower liqueur

430g / 3¼ cups all-purpose flour

Salted butter, for greasing

Apple Mash (page 127)

Elderflower Syrup (recipe follows)

In a large bowl, whisk together the eggs, sugar, and salt. Add the milk and cordial, and stir well. Sift in the flour and stir until you have a smooth batter. Let the batter rest for 30 minutes on the counter.

Heat a large skillet over medium. Once warm, add a small knob of butter. Ladle some batter into the skillet, tilting the skillet to move the mixture around the bottom to create a thin and even layer. Quickly pour any excess batter back into the batter mixture, then return the skillet to the heat. Let cook undisturbed for 30 seconds. Using a spatula, carefully bend a corner of the pancake to see if it's golden on the other side. If it is, flip the pancake and cook until the second side is lightly golden, about 30 seconds. Transfer the pancake to a plate and keep warm until ready to serve. Repeat with the remaining butter and batter. As you continue to cook the pancakes, you may have to reduce the heat.

Spread each pancake with 1 to 2 dollops of Apple Mash, then roll up into a cigar. Serve warm with a generous drizzle of elderflower syrup.

ELDERFLOWER SYRUP

Serves 4 to 6

---

2 tablespoons raw summer honey

4 tablespoons My Mother's Raw Elderflower Cordial (page 184), or a good-quality store-bought elderflower liqueur

---

In a small jar or bowl, combine the honey and cordial. Add more honey for a sweeter mixture, if desired.

BLACKCURRANT PORRIDGE
WITH PEARL BARLEY

Serves 4 to 6

This porridge is a seasonal dessert that you can easily make with whatever berries or fruits you have in your garden or what can be found at the market. Mix different varieties or stick to one kind. I make it with blackcurrants for a velvety, deep-purple porridge. The pearl barley adds a wonderfully soft texture to this simple dessert. Serve warm with a heaping spoonful of double cream and a cup of tea.

150g / ¾ cup pearl barley

750ml / scant 3¼ cups water

35g / ⅓ cup cornstarch

95g / ½ cup sugar, plus more for sprinkling

300g / 2 cups blackcurrants

200ml / ¾ cup plus 1 tablespoon double cream / heavy cream, for serving

Put the barley in a medium saucepan, cover with 300ml / 1¼ cups of water, and bring to a boil over medium-high heat. Boil until tender, 45 to 60 minutes, checking midway and adding more water if necessary. Drain the water and set the barley aside.

In a small bowl, combine 100ml / ⅓ cup of water with the cornstarch until you have a smooth, lump-free liquid.

In a large saucepan set over medium-high heat, combine the remaining 350ml / 1½ cups of water, the sugar, and the blackcurrants, and bring to a boil. Reduce the heat to low and simmer until the currants are soft and almost dissolved, 5 to 6 minutes. Remove the pan from the heat. Strain the liquid into a large bowl, squeezing out all the juice from the blackcurrants through the strainer with the back of a wooden spoon. Discard the blackcurrants.

Pour the cornstarch mixture into the currant liquid in a thin stream, while constantly stirring to avoid lumps. Return the mixture to the pan and place on the stove over medium-high heat. Bring to a boil. Reduce the heat to low and simmer until smooth, 2 to 3 minutes.

Before serving, stir in the barley. Pour the porridge into a serving bowl and sprinkle a thin layer of sugar on top to prevent a film from developing. Serve warm or cold with a spoonful of cream and another sprinkle of sugar.

LIMONCELLO PANNA COTTA WITH PASSION FRUIT

Serves 6 to 8

Having lived and spent a lot of time in Italy over the years, I've been won over by the classic dessert panna cotta time and time again. I love the light zing of limoncello and fresh passion fruit in mine. It keeps well in the fridge and can be made a day in advance. Serve chilled with a sweet dessert wine and generous spoonfuls of fresh passion fruit. I garnish my panna cotta with physalis, a husked nightshade commonly known as Cape gooseberry.

600ml / 2½ cups double cream / heavy cream

150g / scant cup sugar

3 gelatin sheets or 1½ teaspoons powdered gelatin

100ml / ⅓ cup plus 1 tablespoon limoncello, store-bought or homemade (page 70)

3 to 4 fresh passion fruits halved, or 150ml / ½ cup plus 2 tablespoons passion fruit coulis, for garnish

Grated zest of 1 unwaxed lemon, for serving

6 to 8 physalis, for garnish

In a small saucepan set over medium-low heat, bring the cream and sugar to a gentle simmer.

Submerge the gelatin sheets in cold water until soaked and completely softened, 2 to 3 minutes. Scrunch it between your fingers, then add the gelatin to the cream mixture and stir until the gelatin dissolves. If using powdered gelatin, dissolve it in water according to the package instructions before adding it to the cream mixture. Stir in the limoncello. Pour the mixture into 6 to 8 ramekins, depending on the size, and let cool for 15 to 20 minutes.

Cover the ramekins and refrigerate for 1 to 2 hours before serving. Either serve the panna cotta in the ramekins, or quickly dip the bottom of the ramekin in warm water to loosen the panna cotta from the base before turning it upside down onto serving plates.

Top each panna cotta with half a passion fruit or a dollop of passion fruit coulis, a sprinkling of lemon zest, and an open physalis.

BLACKCURRANT AND CINNAMON TODDY

SOLBÆR TODDY

Makes 1L / 4¼ cups

There are few drinks that hold such nostalgic value to me as this one. Growing up, we would pick blackcurrants during summer and autumn and freeze them. Then, when it began snowing outside, my mother would light the fireplace and make this warm drink. It always felt so nurturing, and I would drink it daily, every afternoon, for months, much as I now enjoy a warm cup of tea. Served chilled, either on its own or diluted, it's a lovely summer drink as well, but I suggest you freeze half of the liquid and bring it back to life as the cold and dark winter season sets in. Serve warm, full strength or diluted if you feel it's too strong. In many places this toddy is traditionally served with alcohol; try adding one part Cognac to six or seven parts *solbær*, and serve it warm.

400g / 2⅔ cups blackcurrants

2L / 8½ cups water

4 tablespoons honey

2 cinnamon sticks

In a medium saucepan set over medium heat, combine the blackcurrants and water, cover, and bring to a boil. Reduce the heat to low and simmer until the currants have almost dissolved, about 20 minutes. Press the currants through a piece of cheesecloth. Return the liquid to the saucepan, and add the honey (sweeten with more honey to taste if needed) and cinnamon sticks. Bring to a boil over medium-high heat. Reduce the heat to low and simmer until the liquid is reduced by half, 30 to 40 minutes. Using a spoon, skim and discard the white foam that forms on top of the simmering liquid.

Sterilize (see Tip, page 69) a sufficient number of jars to hold the toddy. Pour the drink into the jars and refrigerate. The drink will keep in an airtight container in the refrigerator for 1 to 2 months.

MY MOTHER'S RAW ELDERFLOWER CORDIAL

Makes 1½ L / 6¼ cups

Preparing elderflower cordial with my mother's recipe preserves all its nutrients, while also enhancing the flavor. The method is perhaps a bit old school, and you do need to tend to it over the course of 14 days, but it's well worth the wait. With its bright yellow color, it's a great cocktail cordial, and I also use it in quite a few recipes in this book. It's a treasured seasonal treat, feels so satisfying to make, and also makes a lovely hostess gift.

100 elderflower flower heads	1kg / 5 cups sugar	Juice of 6 lemons
6 lemons, sliced		

Do not rinse the flowers, but gently shake off any insects. Make sure to break off the thick green stems of the flower bulb (the thin spindly ones are fine to leave attached). In a large ceramic or glass bowl (no aluminum, as the acidity will react with it), layer 15 to 16 flowers. Top with a layer of slices from 1 lemon, about ¾ cup of sugar, and the juice of 1 lemon. Repeat this layering 5 times, finishing with a top layer of sugar. Cover with a lid or plastic wrap and store for 14 days in a cool place—it does not need to be refrigerated—making sure to stir it at least once a day.

After 14 days, sterilize some jars or bottles (see Tip, page 69) sufficiently large to hold the cordial. Strain and pour the liquid into the jars.

To serve, in a glass, combine 40% cordial and 60% water, sparkling water, or prosecco. The syrup will keep in an airtight jar in the refrigerator for up to 10 days.

ROSEWATER AND STRAWBERRY JAM

Makes 350g / 12 ounces

(1 small jar)

My mother makes wonderfully simple jams by quickly stirring together berries and fruit, leaving them with a looser jam consistency than what's familiar to non-Norwegians. We call these types of jam *rårørt*, which means "stirred together raw." You keep much of the fresh fruit flavor making jam this way, but of course it needs to be consumed sooner and, as mentioned, is a tad more loose in consistency. You can omit the rosewater, if you wish, and add vanilla paste for another version of this easy jam. Serve on toast, Norwegian Waffles (page 64), Prosecco Scones (page 280) with Clotted Cream (page 124), freshly baked bread, or over your breakfast porridge. For the best results, be sure to use quality, in-season strawberries. This is a modest recipe, quantity wise, so double or triple it for a larger batch.

500g / 3 cups strawberries, quartered	150g / 1 scant cup caster sugar / superfine sugar	1 teaspoon salted butter 1¼ teaspoons rosewater

In a medium saucepan set over medium-high heat, add the strawberries, sugar, and butter, cover, and bring to a boil. Reduce the heat to low and simmer until the mixture has a loose jam consistency, 30 to 40 minutes. Stir occasionally, giving the strawberries a little bash as you do. Remove the pan from the heat and stir in the rosewater.

Sterilize (see Tip, page 69) 1 or 2 jam jars, depending on the size. Pour the jam into the jars and tighten the lids. The jam will keep in a sterilized airtight jar in a dark cool place for up to 1 month or in the fridge after opening for up to 1 week.

autumn

"I NEED A GREEN HAT with long, elegant pheasant feathers," I told Vanessa, the owner of a clothing shop up the street one afternoon over tea. "Where town meets country," read the sign in her window display, which seemed like a sign made for me.

There comes a time in a woman's life when she needs to invest in a proper coat and hat. And this was that moment. Vanessa nodded from her seat at the other side of the shop counter. "I know just the one," she said, disappearing into the back room. I sipped the steaming cup of Earl Grey tea she'd made me, and looked out the window at the people walking past on their daily errands. I don't remember the first time I met Vanessa, but we quickly became friends after I discovered her little gem of a shop carrying tailored tweed jackets, olive-green wellies with just the right fit, and hats, lots of hats, which all came in their very own red hat box with gold lettering.

"What's the occasion?" she chirped back excitedly as she emerged from the back room with two hats in tow.

"Because it's autumn," I said in all seriousness. "And there comes a time when a woman simply needs to buy an outfit, dress up, and head out on her very own." Vanessa agreed, but I suspect she secretly assumed perhaps a boy was involved. I simply smiled coyly and later carried my hat box and coat with eager steps toward the cottage that same afternoon. With shooting season ahead, and plenty of horse races to attend, I wanted to be prepared. In the words of my mother, you simply never know what might happen, but if you have the outfit ready, you're already halfway there.

AFTER THE FIRST STORM IN AUGUST, summer would not return to Norway until next year. Armed with empty buckets and chipped mugs, my mother would gather the troops to pick the very last of the berries and fruit before the rain knocked them to the ground. My grandmother would pack her little yellow car full of buckets, wellies, hiking sticks, and her silk scarves—finding at least some room for my grandfather as well—and head to our family's old log home in the mountains. And just as the first storm in August marked the end of the berry season in the lowland, it also signaled the time to head up north, where we would forage for wild raspberries, cranberries, blueberries, and the infamous and ever-elusive cloudberry.

A former seamstress, my grandmother had impeccable taste, and represented an era of elegant women who had shoes specially designed for driving, covered their hair in neat silk scarves when berry picking, and always dressed in pressed trousers and a blouse when going for an afternoon stroll. She brewed black coffee on the wood-burning stove at the cabin, made blueberry pancakes for breakfast, and emerged from the mountains all rosy-cheeked and ever so proud. Rarely did she and my grandfather return with anything less than 90kg (about 200 pounds) of ripe wild berries picked between them, filling the trunk of her little car with heaping buckets.

I miss the taste of small wild berries—like the little strawberries that we'd pierce with a straw and make necklaces with before gobbling them down; ocean-blue blueberries, scooped up in wooden mugs that hung from my belt as I helped pick a bucket load. My knees would be blue from kneeling on the crushed berries surrounding the bushes, trying to reach farther and farther in to get every juicy morsel.

During summer and autumn, we spent months in the Norwegian mountains at our family log home that my great-great-grandfather Simen Smiefloden built. Rinsing berries in candlelight at night, with the sweet smell of jam simmering away on the wood-burning stove, the rather humble cottage kitchen would become filled with the comforting aroma of the familiar, and of family tradition. The nearby stream served as our fridge, keeping our butter and milk just cool enough to pour on our morning porridge. However, as soon as the milk showed any signs of going sour, my mother would pour the content into her large cast-iron pot, add a few more logs to the constant fire crackling away in the wood burner, and bring the milk to a boil. As the cheese curds gathered on the top and separated from the milk whey, she'd quickly pour it into a cheesecloth and hang it over the pot until all the liquid had escaped through the tightly woven cloth. Seasoning it with salt and caraway seeds, we'd have fresh cheese for lunch, with bread warm out of the oven. It was magic—but, then again, cooking always is.

WE HAD BEEN STAYING COZY, snug, and comfortably tucked away from the world while getting to know each other, my dog Mr. Whiskey and I. But I could feel the winds change. The heap of recipes scribbled down on any papers that were lying around was piling up on my desk; the cottage kitchen felt crammed with pots and pans; and our little backyard was too small to turn into a proper working garden. It was time to leave our safe nest. We needed a bigger garden to grow our produce, a larger kitchen to work on, and another guest room for all our friends and family who came to stay. One part of me wanted to just pull the covers over my head and stay safely tucked away in this darling cottage on the outskirts of town, yet the voice inside that had previously urged me to change my direction in life had begun whispering of more to come, of a change and growth that stretched beyond these thick old cottage walls. It whispered of being brave, and of standing tall.

"I've found it!" I exclaimed through the phone, with much more gusto in my voice than I had anticipated.

"Where is it?" my mother asked excitedly. I told her about a hamlet tucked away on the outskirts of an ancient woodland on a nearby estate, next to a walled garden and a medieval castle. It had its own garden that stretched all around the house, with a 650-year-old yew tree with a tree house. Its Georgian windows are taller than me, I told her with pride in my voice.

"What about the kitchen?" she wanted to know. "Mum," I began, "it's perfect." With tall ceilings and enough room for an old farm table in the middle, its window overlooking the small herb garden outside, complete with lavender and a bay leaf tree, I could perfectly fit my new gas stove and cook up a feast fit for a king. "It feels like there's room to grow in that house," I told her over the phone, "like I can embark on the next chapter in my life."

"Won't you miss the old cottage?" she asked.

I hesitated before replying, feeling a nudge of sadness at the thought of leaving my safe little nook in the world behind. "I might," I said, "but it's time to move on."

After a week of working in Venice, I returned home to the shire and crossed the border from Dorset to Wiltshire in a moving van. I quickly began hanging up gilded antique mirrors, inviting my girl-friends over to paint the large north-facing living room a dark moody blue, and bought a big vintage French dresser for the smaller south-facing breakfast room. The bottom of the garden housed the ruins of an ancient mausoleum that to my relief had never been consecrated, and the nearby estate—in true *Downton Abbey* style—housed many a tale of a bygone era. I no longer lived on the outskirts of a small English town, but in a quiet hamlet complete with stables and a clock tower.

Every now and then, in the morning, with a gentle fog engulfing the rolling hills in its mystical embrace, I could hear a horn being blown in the distance and the sounds of horses galloping past. Hunting season had begun, and Mr. Whiskey was on edge as flocks of hounds emerged over the hilltop behind our new home at dawn. If someone had told me that I'd one day be living in an old Georgian house in the English countryside with a dog, spending my days cooking, I might have suggested that they were speaking about the wrong person. I had other plans for my life. I'd yet to feel the urge to return to my country-side roots, and I had never really spent any time in England. But that is perhaps the beauty of life, that at a moment's notice one can change the direction one is walking. At any given time we have the tools to turn our lives around, to learn new skills, and to become the person we have the potential to be.

The stove was rarely turned off those first few days in my new home on the estate, with hearty stews bubbling on the stovetop and roasts and baked goods browning in the oven. I brought in large branches from the bay tree in the garden and hung them to dry from the ceil-ing. I began stocking the pantry with spices and teas from my travels, dates and figs for the winter season, and eggs from the neighboring farm, as well as apples from the walled garden on the estate. With the fireplace lit in the dining room, I cored a few of the apples, heated my mother's old cast-iron skillet, and carefully stuffed each apple with golden raisins and chopped almonds. I made sure the sugar and butter

had caramelized in the hot skillet before arranging the apples side by side in the bubbling, dark golden caramel. I knew my mother would make the very same baked apple dessert in her kitchen far away in Norway, and I took comfort in knowing we could be miles apart but united in the kitchen, in spirit nevertheless.

In Norway, when two people who are related are very similar, perhaps in both looks and personality, we say, "The apple doesn't fall very far from the tree." Though my mother and I live in different countries and cook in separate kitchens, we are ever so similar and forever connected. I am my own person, yet it's her voice I hear when I welcome people into my home, her hands I see stirring a pot of slowly simmering stew. I hope that, as the years pass, I'll be even more like her. Through her wonderful example of heartfelt and generous cooking, I'm inspired to do the same, and with this I'm carrying on a tradition of warmth and joy that everyone who comes into her presence can feel.

"It's a daily choice," she told me when I asked her how she does it. "It's a choice, a commitment to being the change you wish to see in the world, because after all, we are the makers of the person we want to be," and a big part of creating the environment we live in. Autumn winds blew, and I wrapped my scarf tighter as I took Mr. Whiskey for his afternoon walk through the woods on the estate.

Be the change you wish to see in the world, I whispered to no one in particular as I watched the tall trees sway in the wind, as if to say, "You've come a long way, little girl."

STARTERS AND SIDES

Autumn Bruschetta
with Chanterelles

Oysters with Basil Sauce

My Potted Crab

Leek and Cheese Gratin

My Mother's Pancakes
with Blueberries

Black Pudding with Scallops
and Caviar

My Mother's Rye Bread

MAINS

Orange and Clove Roast Chicken
with Pears and Butternut Squash

Wild Rabbit and Snail Stew

Steak and Cheese Pie

Grilled Lobster with Lime and
Cilantro Butter

Potato Soup with Smoked Salmon

Shellfish and Tomato Spaghetti

Baked Partridges with Figs
and Olives

DESSERTS

My Mother's Baked Skillet Apples

Crisp Apple Fritters
with Brandy Sauce

Pear and Ginger Tarte Tatin
with Vanilla

My Grandmother's Doughnuts
with Chocolate Sauce

Blackberry and Apple Crumble

DRINKS AND JAM

Sloe Gin

Mulled Cider

My Mother's Plum Jam

AUTUMN BRUSCHETTA
WITH CHANTERELLES

Serves 4

"Chanterelles!" my mother would exclaim with delight upon discovering a wee gathering of them as she scoured the forest in our neighborhood during the wet autumn months. There were whispers in the neighborhood that bountifuls had been found, but no one would spill the beans on where they were. Every family had their own secret spot, and we had ours, although it changed almost every season. Finding these golden treasures felt like stumbling upon a little gold mine. I strongly remember the aroma, the way the kitchen smelled as soon as the mushrooms hit the pan of sizzling butter. We'd all gather around in the kitchen, instantly drawn in by the earthy, sweet, and slightly peppery perfume. It's this nostalgia that motivates me to wade through muddy paths in the woods around my cottage here in England searching for my chanterelles, searching to re-create the edible memories of my childhood. We would eat this simple dish as an evening meal before bedtime, gathering around for the last little meal of the day, and cherishing every bite.

350g / 12 ounces chanterelles

1 tablespoon olive oil

1 tablespoon salted butter, plus more for serving

1 tablespoon double cream / heavy cream

Sea salt and coarsely ground black pepper

4 slices of sourdough bread, for serving

1 garlic clove, halved

Roughly chopped fresh flat-leaf parsley, for garnish (optional)

In a large skillet set over medium heat, heat the olive oil. Add the chanterelles. Do not stir at this point, allowing the chanterelles to fry, but give the skillet a good shake after about 1 minute. Once the mushrooms are cooked through, after 2 to 3 minutes, add the butter and gently swirl it in the skillet until melted. Leave to cook for 1 to 2 minutes before adding the cream. Stir well and season with salt and pepper to taste.

Toast the bread slices, rub with the garlic halves, and spread each slice with butter. Serve the bread on a platter with some warm chanterelle mixture spooned onto each slice. If desired, garnish with parsley.

OYSTERS WITH BASIL SAUCE

Serves 2

I cried the very first time I had oysters. Seated in an overcrowded restaurant in an American desert town, with dodgy seafood to say the least, my date for the evening persuaded me to order "fresh" oysters. We spent the evening chatting away like old friends, ingesting with great gusto the open oysters nestled in ice on the table between us. He was tall and charming, a gentleman who read books and studied English literature, and I loved our conversation. As we finished the meal, not knowing where to put my hands, I picked up an empty oyster shell from a pile next to my plate, lifted it up close to my face and inhaled the salty smell of the sea. Catching me completely by surprise, tears welled up in my eyes and I let out a high-pitched cry. The expression on my date's face was priceless—he instantly leaned back with a bewildered frown on his face. I tried to explain, between loud breathing noises as I sobbed into my napkin, that it smelled like home. It had a scent like the soft ocean breeze of our island in Norway. My date and I may have ended up as friends, but my love for oysters had only just begun.

Oysters from off the coast of Scotland are terrific and have a slight mineral taste, and I adore oysters from Cornwall. If you have the chance to visit northern Denmark, you can rent a wading outfit and wellies, load your rucksack with champagne, and, armed with a shucking knife, scour the coastline and eat as many as you'd like! I like mine raw, usually just with a squeeze of fresh lemon juice and a drop or two of Tabasco, but when friends come over for a seafood dinner, this is my go-to recipe, fresh and simple.

1 tablespoon finely chopped fresh basil	A good pinch of crushed red pepper flakes	8 oysters, shucked (shells reserved) or unshucked
2 tablespoons olive oil	Coarsely ground black pepper	½ lemon, seeded

In a food processor or blender, blend the basil, olive oil, red pepper flakes, and black pepper until smooth. Alternatively, finely chop the basil and whisk it together with the oil, red pepper flakes, and black pepper.

You can ask your fishmonger to open the oysters for you, or you can freshly shuck them with a small knife or an oyster shucker. To open them yourself, wrap an oyster in a towel and hold the oyster firmly on a flat surface. Insert the dull tip of an oyster knife between the shell halves where the muscle is located, and gently wiggle the knife to open the oyster, working your way from one side to the other as you pry it open. Once open, run the knife underneath the oyster to detach it from the muscle completely, but leave it in its shell (take care not to cut the meat itself).

Spoon the basil mixture over the oysters, squeeze the lemon on top, and serve immediately.

MY POTTED CRAB

Makes 500g / 17 ounces

My first year in England was often spent down by the stunning coast off the Isle of Purbeck. There, among rolling green hills and white cliffs where sheep graze peacefully, is a sleepy little village with a thatched roof café called Clavell's. This is where I had potted shrimp for the first time. There was nothing not to love about it. Spread on toast, the cool, spiced butter sauce with salty shrimp felt like everything I loved all in one, combined in a new simple way. I still go there for its potted shrimp, among other wonderful things on the menu, and its owners have become dear friends. When trying to make it in my own kitchen, I found that the creamy texture of crab and a few spices familiar to my Norwegian heritage bridged the two worlds together beautifully, and this has become my version, my potted crab. This spread is lovely as a starter on toast, or as a lunch snack with a green side salad.

150g / ⅔ cup (1 stick plus scant 4 tablespoons) salted butter

4 anchovies, in olive oil

Zest of 1 unwaxed lemon

4 teaspoons fresh lemon juice

2 to 3 cardamom pods, shelled and finely ground

1 teaspoon coarsely ground black pepper

½ teaspoon crushed red pepper flakes

Scant ⅓ teaspoon ground cumin

Scant ⅓ teaspoon ground nutmeg

200g / 7 ounces white crab meat

100g / 4 ounces brown crab meat

1 teaspoon sea salt

In a small saucepan set over medium-low heat, melt two-thirds of the butter. Add the anchovies, lemon zest and juice, cardamom, black pepper, red pepper flakes, cumin, and nutmeg. Remove the pan from the heat and set aside to infuse for 10 minutes.

Stir the crabmeat and salt into the butter mixture. Place the mixture in a ramekin or divide between 2 or more ramekins, depending on the size, filling them two-thirds from the top. Melt the remaining butter and pour it over the top to seal in the crab mixture, dividing the butter among the ramekins. Refrigerate for 7 hours before serving. Serve within 24 hours.

LEEK AND CHEESE GRATIN

Serves 8

My dear friend Heather Whitehead, who bakes the most naughtily delicious cakes for a living, made this leek and cheese gratin for one of my food and photography workshops hosted in my home in the English countryside, and I almost licked my plate clean after eating it. It's a wonderful side for almost any meat dish, and is the kind of comfort food that cold weather makes you yearn for. Serve warm out of the oven, making sure there's enough for everyone to have a second helping.

---

4 large leeks, cut in half lengthwise, cleaned well, and sliced

1 tablespoon unsalted butter

1 tablespoon olive oil

1 heaping teaspoon all-purpose flour

100ml / ⅓ cup plus 1 tablespoon single cream

100ml / ⅓ cup plus 1 tablespoon whole milk

100g / 1¼ cups grated Parmesan

5 fresh thyme sprigs, leaves finely chopped

Sea salt and coarsely ground black pepper

100g / 1 cup fresh bread crumbs

Preheat the oven to 170°C / 340°F.

In a medium saucepan set over medium heat, gently cook the leeks in the butter and oil, stirring occasionally, until softened, 5 minutes. Stir in the flour and cook for 1 minute. Pour in the cream and milk, stir until smooth, and let simmer for 1 minute. Remove the pan from the heat, stir in the cheese and thyme, and season with salt and pepper to taste. Spoon the mixture into a shallow gratin dish and scatter with the bread crumbs.

Bake until golden and bubbling, 30 minutes.

MY MOTHER'S PANCAKES
WITH BLUEBERRIES

Makes 18 to 20 pancakes

The comforting smell of homemade pancakes wafting through the house fills me with childhood memories. This traditional recipe is a quintessential example of my mother's familiar, nostalgic, and simple cooking. Uncomplicated and gently flavored, these paper-thin pancakes can be made for breakfast, lunch, or dinner, and are traditionally served with mashed fresh blueberries and a sprinkling of sugar spread on the inside of the pancake before being rolled up into a cigar shape. Another lovely way to serve them, especially during summer, is with fresh strawberries and drizzled with caramel sauce (page 130).

4 medium eggs	800ml / 3⅓ cups water	600g / 4 cups fresh blueberries, for serving
1 tablespoon sugar	160g / 1¼ cups all-purpose flour	
1 teaspoon sea salt	Salted butter, for greasing	

In a large bowl, whisk together the eggs, sugar, and salt. Add the water and whisk well. Sift in the flour and stir well until the batter is smooth; use a whisk if necessary. Any small lumps will disappear after resting. Let the batter rest for 30 minutes on the counter. The batter may be stored, covered, overnight in the refrigerator and used the next day after being brought to room temperature. (I usually take it out 30 minutes before cooking.)

Heat a large skillet over medium. Once warm, add a small knob of butter. Ladle some batter into the skillet, tilting the skillet to move the mixture around the base to create a thin, even layer. Quickly pour any excess batter back into the batter mixture, then return the skillet to the heat. Let the batter cook undisturbed for 30 seconds. Using a spatula, carefully bend a corner of the pancake to see if it's golden on the other side. If it is, flip the pancake and cook until the second side is lightly golden, about 30 seconds. Transfer the pancake to a plate and keep warm until ready to serve. Repeat with the remaining butter and batter. You may have to reduce the heat.

To serve, roll the pancakes into cigars and divide among individual plates, along with the fresh blueberries.

BLACK PUDDING
WITH SCALLOPS AND CAVIAR

Serves 4 to 5

Black pudding was a readily available everyday food in Norway for my mother and grandmother; however, food traditions have changed a lot since then. I wasn't introduced to it until I had my first full English breakfast with extra bacon and mushrooms next to sausages and scrambled eggs, after moving to England. Spicy and full of flavor, black pudding has certainly made it into my cottage kitchen pantry. Paired with scallops and topped with caviar, this humble pudding is given a luxurious makeover, and the combination of flavors are a match made in heaven. Serve warm and enjoy with a chilled glass of cloudy cider.

---

1 tablespoon plus 1 teaspoon salted butter

200g / 7 ounces chopped slab pancetta or cured bacon lardons

110g / 4 ounces black pudding, sliced 1½cm / ½ inch thick

10 fresh scallops

2 tablespoons black lumpfish caviar

Preheat the oven to 100°C / 210°F.

Heat a large skillet over medium. Add 1 tablespoon of butter, and when it sizzles add the pancetta. Fry the pancetta until golden and crisp, 4 to 5 minutes. Transfer to a small bowl and put it in the oven keep warm.

Add the black pudding slices to the warm skillet with the pancetta fat in it. Cook until crisp and cooked through, 4 to 6 minutes per side. Transfer them to a plate and keep warm in the oven.

In a large clean skillet set over medium heat, add the remaining teaspoon of butter. When it sizzles, add the scallops and cook until seared and just cooked through, 2 to 3 minutes per side.

Arrange a slice of black pudding on each serving plate, then place a scallop on top of the black pudding. Sprinkle with pancetta and top each scallop with caviar. Serve immediately.

MY MOTHER'S RYE BREAD

Makes 4 rings

The last time my father visited me here in England, he mentioned that he used to buy this type of rye bread at the local deli when he was growing up in Oslo. The round loaves would all be arranged on a pole hanging from the ceiling. He grew quite nostalgic when my mother and I baked him a batch, even if Mum has done so for years. There are many types of rye bread, and this is the one I crave the most, as it has this lovely and unexpected aroma of star anise that works so well with rye. You can substitute caraway seeds for the anise, if you wish, as either one will enhance this humble bread. Eat it warm, slicing each ring horizontally through the middle and slathering it with butter, or serve it beside a bowl of soup. When cooled, wrap the bread in a kitchen towel to enjoy later; it will keep for 2 to 3 days.

---

4 tablespoons salted butter, plus more for greasing

350ml / 1½ cups whole milk

2 tablespoons light golden syrup (available at Amazon.com)

2 to 3 teaspoons ground anise

400g / 3 cups coarse rye flour

200g / 1½ cups all-purpose flour, plus more for rolling

4 teaspoons active dry yeast

2 teaspoons sea salt

In a small saucepan, melt the butter with the milk over medium-low heat, making sure it does not boil or bubble. Remove from the heat, add the syrup, and mix well. Allow the mixture to cool to skin temperature (about 37°C / 95°F). Test a drop on the back of your hand to feel if it's the right temperature.

In a large mixing bowl, combine the anise, rye and all-purpose flours, yeast, and salt, then stir in the warm milk mixture. Knead the dough with your hands in the bowl until the stickiness is gone and it feels firm and tender to the touch, 4 to 6 minutes. Lift the dough, sprinkle a bit of flour into the bottom of the bowl, then put the dough back in, covering the bowl with a kitchen towel. Leave to rise in a warm draft-free place for 1 to 1½ hours, until doubled in size. Lightly flour a surface, empty the dough onto it, and knead for 2 to 3 minutes, adding more flour if needed.

Preheat the oven to 200°C / 400°F.

recipe continues

Divide the dough into 4 equal parts, shape each part into a ball before rolling into 20-centimeter / 8-inch disks that are ¾-inch-thick. Cut out a 5-centimeter / 2-inch circle in the middle of each disk with a small glass or something equivalent. Brush the surface and edges of the dough disks with cold water. Butter 2 large baking sheets large enough to hold the dough disks. Place two bread disks on each sheet, about 8 cm / 3 inches apart, and arrange the circle cut-outs alongside them. Use a fork to prick the bread surface generously and let rise for another 30 minutes. Bake until lightly golden, 10 to 15 minutes.

ORANGE AND CLOVE
ROAST CHICKEN WITH
PEARS AND BUTTERNUT SQUASH

Serves 4

Everyone has a go-to roast chicken recipe, and this is mine. The combination of clove and orange creates a wonderful aroma, and, paired with butternut squash and pears, it's a terrific meal. As it uses only one pot, this dish is easy and relatively quick to make, and is just as delicious reheated the next day, or made into a chicken soup with whatever is left over. Put it in the oven an hour before your guests arrive, and you'll have time for a stress-free cocktail before enjoying the main meal.

50g / ¼ cup unsalted butter, room temperature, plus more for greasing

1 (1.8kg / 4 pounds) free-range organic chicken

½ teaspoon coarsely ground black pepper, plus more for seasoning

¼ teaspoon crushed red pepper flakes

Sea salt

1 teaspoon whole cloves

2 oranges, quartered

5 to 7 fresh thyme sprigs

2 to 3 fresh sage sprigs

4 garlic cloves, crushed, skin-on

1.3kg / 2.9 pounds butternut squash, peeled, cored, cut in half lengthwise, and sliced

2 yellow onions, quartered

1kg / 2.2 pounds British Mans Piper potatoes (Yukon Gold will also work), peeled and quartered

4 Conference pears or other firm pears, halved and cored

Extra-virgin olive oil, for roasting

240ml / 1 cup white wine

Preheat the oven to 200°C / 400°F with a rack set in the middle.

Butter a large roasting pan with 3-centimeter / 1¼-inch-high sides. Remove the chicken from the fridge 30 minutes prior to roasting. Pat the chicken dry with a paper towel. Place the chicken in the prepared roasting pan, breast-side up.

Using a mortar and pestle, firmly pound the butter, black pepper, and red pepper flakes until well combined. Use your hand to carefully loosen the skin away from the chicken breast. Gently stuff half of the butter mixture underneath the skin on the back of the chicken. Rub the remaining butter over the

recipe continues

top of the chicken, then season generously with salt and black pepper. Press the whole cloves into the top of the chicken, piercing the skin with the clove tip or with a skewer. Squeeze 2 orange wedges over the top of the chicken. Place 2 additional orange wedges inside the chicken with half of the thyme, sage, and garlic.

Arrange the butternut squash, onion quarters, potatoes, pears, and remaining orange wedges around the chicken, and scatter the remaining thyme, sage, and garlic among the vegetables. Liberally drizzle with olive oil and half of the wine. Cover with aluminum foil.

Place the pan on the middle rack of the oven. Roast 30 to 35 minutes. Remove the pan from the oven, uncover, and stir the vegetables well every 10 minutes. Baste the chicken with the juices from the pan and the rest of the white wine. Reduce the oven temperature to 180°C / 350°F and roast, uncovered, until the chicken is cooked through and crispy brown, stirring through twice more, 20 to 25 minutes.

WILD RABBIT AND SNAIL STEW

Serves 6

Ducking into a small family-run restaurant in Madrid on a cold autumn day, after having spent hours perusing the city's treasured art collections in the Prado and Reina Sofia—that's my kind of heaven. Admiring art and strolling in and out of the charming streets of this old city always makes me work up quite an appetite. I love a good stew on a cold day, and after being introduced to the flavors of Spanish cooking during my trips to the city while working as a flight attendant for Scandinavian Airlines, I fell in love with this hearty dish. Serve piping hot with buttered sourdough bread, Rosemary Breadsticks (page 92), or No-Knead Country Loaf (page 32) to mop up the juices, and a dry red wine or cider.

---

1 tablespoon plus 1 teaspoon salted butter

150ml / ½ cup plus 1 tablespoon olive oil

2 whole rabbits, or 1½kg / 3½ pounds of legs and fillets from 2 rabbits

3 to 4 fresh or 250 to 300g / 8 to 10 ounces roasted paprika peppers / red bell peppers

2 to 4 garlic cloves, halved

2 to 3 shallots, sliced

6 to 8 fresh rosemary sprigs, leaves finely chopped

2 dried bay leaves

Sea salt and coarsely ground black pepper

600ml / 2½ cups dry apple cider

1 bottle dry white wine

200g / 7 ounces snails, in shell

Sourdough bread, for serving

In a large skillet set over medium heat, melt 1 tablespoon of butter with 1 tablespoon of oil. Add the rabbit pieces and cook, turning, until the meat is browned on all sides, 2 to 3 minutes total. Transfer to a plate and set aside.

If using fresh peppers, preheat the broiler. Place the peppers on a baking sheet and broil until the skins are completely black and charred, regularly turning them to ensure all sides blacken evenly, 10 to 15 minutes. Let the peppers cool. Remove the charred skins and seeds from the peppers and slice into strips. (If using roasted peppers from a jar, skip this step.)

In a large saucepan set over medium heat, melt the remaining teaspoon of butter. Add the garlic, shallots, rosemary, and bay leaves, and sauté, stirring, 2 to 3 minutes. Add the rabbit and the remaining ½ cup of oil, and season liberally with salt and black pepper. Pour in the cider and wine, and bring to a boil. Reduce the heat to medium-low, cover, and simmer until the rabbit is tender, about 50 minutes. Uncover and add the peppers to the stew, simmering 15 minutes more to combine all the flavors. Add the snails in their shells and simmer until cooked through, about 5 minutes. Serve immediately with sourdough bread.

TIP: When purchasing the rabbits, ask your butcher to cut them into small pieces for you.

STEAK AND CHEESE PIE

Serves 4 to 6

One time, as I was preparing my traditional steak and ale pie, my friend Peter told me to add some cheese to it, the way they do in New Zealand. But I went about making my savory pie the way I always had, until the day my local deli received a big chunk of Taleggio, one of my most treasured cheeses. I went home that afternoon with the whole piece, decided to take my friend's word for it, and added a healthy amount to my steak pie. It was a delicious addition. Needless to say, I invited that same friend over for dinner and shared my creation. "Better than the ones in New Zealand!" he cooed, and I think I fell for him a little that day. This pie is most flavorful if you cook the meat filling a day ahead. While it's delicious on its own, I also like to serve it with Parsnip and Cardamom Puree (page 114) or Mustard Coleslaw (page 40).

---

2 tablespoons salted butter, plus more for greasing

2 tablespoons olive oil

2 to 3 garlic cloves, chopped

700g / 1½ pounds stewing beef, cut into 2½cm / 1-inch cubes

350ml / 1½ cups chicken stock

1 medium yellow onion, chopped

2 tablespoons all-purpose flour

150ml / ½ cup plus 2 tablespoons dry white wine

1½ tablespoons dried porcini mushrooms, roughly chopped

3 to 4 fresh thyme sprigs, leaves chopped

1 tablespoon chopped fresh sage leaves

2 dried bay leaves

230g / 8 ounces frozen puff pastry, thawed

200g / 7 ounces Taleggio cheese, chopped

Preheat the oven to 180°C / 350°F.

In a large ovenproof saucepan set over medium heat, melt the butter with 1 tablespoon of oil. Working in batches, add the garlic and the cubed beef and brown the meat on all sides, 3 to 4 minutes. Transfer to a plate to rest. Add a splash of the stock, scraping up the browned bits on the bottom of the pan, and cook until evaporated, 1 to 2 minutes. Add the remaining tablespoon of oil and the onion and cook, stirring, until lightly transparent, 2 to 3 minutes. Stir in the flour and cook until golden and nutty, about 3 minutes. Add the stock, wine, mushrooms, thyme, sage, and bay leaves and bring to a boil. Return the

recipe continues

meat to the pan, cover, and place the pan in the oven. Bake until the meat is tender, about 1½ hours. At this point, you may let the pie filling cool, then cover and refrigerate overnight. When ready to assemble, remove the meat from the refrigerator and allow it to reach room temperature.

Preheat the oven to 180°C / 350°F. Butter a 24-centimeter / 9½-inch round pie dish with a depth of 4 centimeters / 1½ inches.

On a lightly floured work surface, roll out the pastry into 2 circles large enough to fit the pie dish. Place a circle in the bottom of the pie dish. Add the meat filling and cheese pieces in 3 to 4 layers. Cover the dish with the remaining pastry, trim, and decorate, if desired. Cut a hole in the middle of the pie to allow steam to escape.

Bake until browned on top and heated through, 40 to 55 minutes. If the pastry browns too quickly, cover with foil. Serve hot straight out of oven.

GRILLED LOBSTER WITH
LIME AND CILANTRO BUTTER

Serves 4

All you need for this simple yet luxurious feast is a good fishmonger to source the very best lobsters for you. Paired with fresh basil and coriander butter, this meal is full of flavor. Before preparing them, give the lobsters a quick piercing through the back of the head so they are in fact dead, and plan for one lobster per person. I like serving bubbles with my lobster in true festive fashion, but a crisp white wine will do as well.

4 live lobsters

8 tablespoons finely chopped fresh coriander / cilantro

Zest of 3 unwaxed limes

Juice of ½ lime

250g / 1⅓ cups salted butter, room temperature

3 teaspoons harissa

Sea salt and coarsely ground black pepper

55g / ⅓ cup melted salted butter for brushing

Parsley Buttered Potatoes (recipe follows)

Place the lobsters in the freezer for a couple of hours to sedate them.

In a mortar and pestle or a large bowl, combine the cilantro, lime zest and juice, butter, harissa, and salt and pepper to taste.

Place each lobster on a cutting board, stomach down, and split in half lengthwise with a cleaver, from the head to the tail. Rinse off the yellow-green paste under cold water.

Preheat a grill or the broiler to high.

Lightly brush each lobster with melted butter. When the grill or broiler is hot, place the lobsters flesh-side down on the grill (or broiler rack) and cook for 2 to 3 minutes. Flip the lobsters over and slather them with the lime and cilantro butter, then season with salt and pepper. Grill (or broil) until cooked through, about 5 minutes. Serve with Parsley Buttered Potatoes.

TIP: The zingy and fresh cilantro butter is excellent on top of a good steak, too.

PARSLEY BUTTERED POTATOES

Serves 4

650g / 1 pound new potatoes, scrubbed

Sea salt and coarsely ground black pepper

2 tablespoons salted butter

1 to 2 tablespoons finely chopped fresh flat-leaf parsley, plus more for garnish

---

Put the potatoes in a medium saucepan, cover with water, salt generously, and set the pan over medium-high heat. Bring to a boil and cook until tender, 20 to 25 minutes. Drain the potatoes and put them in a large bowl.

In a small bowl, combine the butter and parsley. Add the butter mixture to the drained potatoes. Toss to coat the potatoes evenly and season generously with salt and a little bit of pepper. Serve warm garnished with parsley.

POTATO SOUP
WITH SMOKED SALMON

Serves 4

My mother taught me to make a creamy and smooth potato soup, which never failed to nourish when I was a young girl. This version came about one day when I was craving her cooking and wanted to bring the warmth of her kitchen into the cottage. The smoked salmon is a must, and so are the croutons, which elevate this quiet yet comforting soup. Serve warm with a dry white wine or a cloudy dry cider.

400g / 14 ounces British Maris Piper potatoes (Yukon Gold will also work), peeled and diced

1 tablespoon salted butter

1 celery stalk, chopped

1 yellow onion, chopped

2 garlic cloves, finely chopped

400ml / 1⅔ cups vegetable stock

350ml / 1½ cups whole milk

¼ teaspoon ground nutmeg

Sea salt and coarsely ground black pepper

1 to 2 tablespoons roughly chopped fresh flat-leaf parsley

100g / 3½ ounces smoked salmon, shaved, for garnish

Croutons (recipe follows), for garnish

Chopped fresh chives, for garnish

Place the potatoes in a medium saucepan, cover with water, and set over high heat. Bring to a boil and cook until tender, 15 to 18 minutes. Drain the potatoes and put them in a bowl; return the empty saucepan to the stove. Mash the potatoes and set aside.

Set the saucepan over medium heat. Melt the butter, then add the celery, onion, and garlic. Sauté, stirring, until the vegetables are soft but not browned, 5 to 10 minutes.

In a separate medium saucepan set over medium-low heat, bring the stock to a boil. Add the hot stock, milk, and nutmeg to the onion mixture, and season with salt and pepper. Add the mashed potatoes and stir well. Bring to a boil, then lower the heat and simmer for 2 to 3 minutes, until it reaches your desired thickness. Stir the parsley into the soup just before serving.

Serve in individual bowls with smoked salmon shavings, croutons, and a sprinkling of chives.

CROUTONS

Makes 100g / 1 cup

---

1 tablespoon salted butter | 100g / 1 cup diced sourdough or other standard bread | Sea salt and coarsely ground black pepper

---

In a large skillet set over medium-low heat, melt the butter. Add the bread and cook, turning the pieces every so often, until lightly browned and crisp on all sides, 8 to 10 minutes total. Season with salt and pepper to taste. Let cool.

TIP: For a lovely alternative, use half a loaf of My Mother's Rye Bread (page 211), cut into 1-centimeter / ⅓-inch cubes, in place of your standard bread.

SHELLFISH AND TOMATO SPAGHETTI

Serves 2

When in need of a special dinner for two, this flavorful dish is a good pick, as it has great character. Mussels are some of my favorite seafood, and I cook with them often, usually giving them a quick steam in cider, butter, garlic, and cream. But every now and then I desire a tomato base for them, and to toss them with other seafood and spaghetti that you can slurp with great gusto. Serve warm with a blushing rosé or dry white wine.

1 tablespoon salted butter

200ml / ¾ cup plus 1 tablespoon dry white wine

150g / 5 ounces fresh clams, in shell, rinsed and scrubbed

300g / 10 ounces fresh mussels, in shell, rinsed and scrubbed

150g / 5 ounces spaghetti

4 tablespoons extra-virgin olive oil

2 to 3 garlic cloves, finely chopped

4 shallots, finely chopped

1 celery stalk, finely chopped

½ fennel bulb, finely chopped

300g / 10 ounces canned plum tomatoes, chopped, drained and juices reserved

250g / 8 ounces raw or pre-boiled prawns, peeled and deveined

Sea salt and coarsely ground black pepper

2 tablespoons chopped fresh cilantro, for garnish

In a large saucepan, with a lid, set over medium heat, combine the butter, wine, clams, and mussels. Cover and cook 4 to 5 minutes, until the mussels and clams have opened, discarding any that haven't. Transfer the shellfish to a large bowl and set aside. Strain the cooking liquid and set aside.

In a separate large saucepan of boiling salted water, cook the spaghetti according to the package instructions until al dente.

Meanwhile, in the same saucepan used to cook the clams and mussels, combine the oil, garlic, shallots, celery, and fennel over medium heat. Cook, stirring, 1 to 2 minutes. Add the tomatoes, reserved juice, and the strained shellfish cooking liquid to the pan, reduce the heat to medium-low and bring to a gentle simmer. Add the mussels, clams, and prawns and cook until the prawns are heated through, 2 to 3 minutes (if using pre-boiled prawns, reduce the cooking time to 1 minute). Add the spaghetti and toss gently. Season with salt and pepper to taste. Garnish with cilantro and serve immediately.

BAKED PARTRIDGES
WITH FIGS AND OLIVES

Serves 4

When I first moved to the cottage, I perused the local market often, searching for fresh ingredients to experiment with in the kitchen. Rabbit, pheasant, and quail were often on display, as was partridge, which I've come to really love. It's like a small chicken with wonderful flavors of the countryside, and you can serve each guest one bird, making a beautiful presentation. Flavor-wise, this dish has notes of rustic Italian cuisine. I often pair it with my favorite Amarone della Valpolicella wine.

---

4 chicken livers, chopped

1 yellow onion, finely chopped

200g / 7 ounces slab pancetta, chopped

2 dried bay leaves

1 tablespoon extra-virgin olive oil

½ teaspoon finely ground fresh juniper berries

70ml / scant ⅓ cup Vin Santo or Marsala wine

500ml / 2 cups plus 2 tablespoons beef stock

Sea salt and freshly ground pepper

4 partridges

8 slices of cured bacon

1 tablespoon salted butter, melted, for brushing

200g / 7 ounces fresh figs, quartered

250g / 8½ ounces pitted green olives

Preheat the oven to 170°C / 340°F.

In a large saucepan set over medium heat, combine the livers, onion, pancetta, bay leaves, olive oil, and juniper berries. Cook until the livers are cooked through, 2 to 3 minutes. Add the wine and stock, and bring to a boil. Reduce the heat to low and cook until reduced by one-third, 25 to 30 minutes. Season with salt and pepper.

Sprinkle the partridges with salt and pepper and wrap each one with 2 slices of bacon, tucking the ends underneath each bird. Brush with the melted butter and place in a large baking dish. Pour the stock mixture over the birds.

Bake, basting with the stock after 15 minutes, until golden, 30 to 35 minutes. Add the figs and olives, stir, and bake until the partridges are fully cooked, 5 to 6 minutes. Arrange the partridges on a serving dish with the figs and olives, drizzle the pan juice over top, and serve.

MY MOTHER'S BAKED SKILLET APPLES

Serves 6

Nothing smells more like autumn than when my mother heats up a skillet and makes a batch of apples with cinnamon, raisins, and almonds. The sugar caramelizes into a golden liquid at the bottom of the skillet, where it blends with the juices of the apples, creating a thick sauce that I scoop over each apple right before serving. Serve piping hot with vanilla ice cream or My Mother's Whipped Cream (page 125), adding ½ teaspoon of orange blossom syrup to the cream mixture before whipping. I use cooking apples in this recipe, but you can use any red or green apple you prefer, depending on how tart you wish it to be. Firm apples hold their shape better than softer ones, which become a mash, but either consistency tastes heavenly.

115g / ½ cup caster sugar / superfine sugar	50g / ⅓ cup roughly chopped almonds or walnuts	70g / ⅔ cup sultanas / golden raisins
2 teaspoons ground cinnamon	Zest of 1 unwaxed orange	6 medium, firm cooking apples, cored and unpeeled

Place half of the sugar in a medium bowl. Add the cinnamon, almonds, orange zest, and raisins, and stir well.

Place a medium skillet over medium heat. Sprinkle the remaining sugar in the skillet in an even layer. Arrange the apples in the pan on top of the sugar, and fill the space where the apples' core used to be with the almond and raisin mixture, scattering the remaining mixture over the apples before placing a lid on the skillet. Cook, monitoring it closely so the sugar doesn't burn, until the apples are tender and soft, 10 to 15 minutes. Serve hot or warm.

CRISP APPLE FRITTERS
WITH BRANDY SAUCE

Makes 15 to 20 fritters

My friends simply can't get enough of this dessert, served warm with a dollop of brandy-spiked sauce, so I usually double the recipe. It has comforting notes of autumn, with apples, cinnamon, and brandy. This dish has quite a short shelf life, so be sure to enjoy it immediately while the fritters are still crisp and lovely. I usually pair it with little glasses of the brandy I use in the sauce.

80g / ¼ cup plus 2 tablespoons granulated sugar

1 tablespoon ground cinnamon

60ml / ¼ cup apple cider

80ml / ⅓ cup double cream / heavy cream

1 medium egg

150g / 1¼ cups self-rising flour

2 tablespoons light brown sugar

½ teaspoon sea salt

1½L / 6⅓ cups vegetable oil

1 to 2 bread crumbs, for testing the oil

5 Granny Smith apples, peeled, cored, and cut into 1½cm / ½-inch-thick disks

Confectioners' sugar, for dusting

Vanilla ice cream, for serving

Brandy Sauce (recipe follows), for serving

In a small bowl, stir together the granulated sugar and cinnamon.

In a large bowl, combine the cider, cream, egg, flour, brown sugar, and salt. The batter should be thick. Let rest on the counter for 15 minutes.

In a large saucepan set over medium-high, heat the frying oil to 180°C / 350°F, using a thermometer to monitor it. To test the oil, toss in a bread crumb. If it turns golden, the oil is ready, but if it burns, the oil is too hot.

Toss the apple disks in the batter to coat. Working in batches, carefully lower 1 to 2 coated disks into the oil and fry, turning frequently, until golden brown, 3 to 4 minutes. Drain on paper towels and sprinkle immediately with the sugar and cinnamon mixture.

When all of the fritters are fried, arrange them on a platter and sprinkle with confectioners' sugar. Serve immediately with ice cream and a generous amount of brandy sauce.

BRANDY SAUCE

Makes 150ml / ½ cup

---

2 tablespoons unsalted butter

120ml / ½ cup double cream / heavy cream

85g / ½ cup packed light brown sugar

2 tablespoons brandy

In a medium saucepan set over medium heat, combine the butter, cream, and sugar. Bring to a boil, reduce the heat to medium-low, and simmer until thickened, 5 to 8 minutes. Remove the pan from the heat and add the brandy. Stir well. Serve hot or cold.

PEAR AND GINGER TARTE TATIN WITH VANILLA

Serves 4 to 6

Outside my cottage is a small pear tree, so laden with fruit in autumn that its branches nearly touch the ground. The pears are quite firm to the touch and hold their shape well when poached in caramel sauce and baked in a tarte tatin. I keep puff pastry in the fridge just in case I want to whip this up for impromptu dinner parties, and I always grate fresh ginger straight into the bubbling, dark-golden caramel to add a little spice to the sweetness. This classic requires little skill, but you will need a dash of self-control not to dip your finger into the bubbling caramel for a cheeky taste!

130g / ⅔ cup caster sugar / superfine sugar

3 tablespoons salted butter, cut into cubes, plus more for greasing

1 tablespoon peeled, grated fresh ginger

1 teaspoon vanilla paste

Juice of ½ lemon

5 Conference pears (or Bartlett or D'Anjou), peeled, cored, and quartered

All-purpose flour, for dusting

170g / 6 ounces frozen puff pastry, thawed

Preheat the oven to 200°C / 400°F. Butter a 20-centimeter / 8-inch pie dish.

In a medium saucepan set over medium heat, melt the sugar and let it cook undisturbed until it becomes golden in color, 3 to 4 minutes. Add the butter, ginger, vanilla paste, and lemon juice. Cook, stirring, until smooth and thick, about 10 minutes. Remove the pan from the heat.

Stir the pears gently into the caramel sauce, then transfer to the prepared pie dish, arranging the pears in a single layer, curved sides down.

On a lightly floured work surface, roll out the sheet of puff pastry. Cut out a circular piece large enough to cover the pie dish. Place the puff pastry sheet over the pears, tucking it snugly under the inside edge of the dish.

Bake until the puff pastry is golden brown, about 30 minutes. Let cool slightly.

Firmly press a large serving plate over the top of the tart and gently flip the plate and pie dish over. Remove the pie dish, releasing the tart. Serve warm.

MY GRANDMOTHER'S DOUGHNUTS WITH CHOCOLATE SAUCE

SMULTRING

Makes 12 to 15 doughnuts

My grandmother kept her doughnuts stored in a tin container in her cupboard, ready to serve whenever we needed a little sweet treat when visiting. She enjoyed them cold with a cup of black coffee in the afternoon. She never wrote down her recipe, and I've been yearning to re-create it ever since she passed away a few years back. With many letters and phone calls between my mother and me, this is where we ended up, as close as we could possibly get to my grandmother's version. These are quite different than Krispy Kreme— and Dunkin' Donut—style doughnuts. They will keep in an airtight container for a few days, but I love them warm, drizzled with my mother's thick and glossy chocolate sauce.

---

2 medium eggs

125g / ½ cup sugar

75ml / ⅓ cup double cream / heavy cream

75ml / ⅓ cup kefir or plain unsweetened yogurt

450g / 3⅓ cups all-purpose flour

1 teaspoon baking powder

1 teaspoon bicarb soda / baking soda

½ teaspoon ground cardamom

2 tablespoons salted butter, melted

1½L / 6⅓ cups vegetable oil

My Mother's Chocolate Sauce, warmed (recipe follows)

In a large bowl, whisk the eggs with the sugar for 8 to 10 minutes, until they reach a light, frothy, meringue-like consistency. In a medium bowl, whisk the cream until soft peaks form and fold into the egg and sugar mixture. Add the kefir / yogurt and stir to combine. Sift in the flour, baking powder, baking soda, and add the cardamom. Add the melted butter to the mixture and stir to combine into a dough. Cover and let rest overnight in the fridge.

The next day, remove the dough from fridge. On a floured surface, use a rolling pin to roll it out to 1 centimeter / ⅓ inch thick. Use an 8-centimeter / 3-inch

recipe continues

doughnut cutter or a glass to cut out circles, then use a smaller 4-centimeter / 1½-inch doughnut cutter or glass to make the hole in the middle.

In a medium saucepan, with a lid, set over medium-high, heat oil to 180°C / 350°F. Test the temperature by dropping the handle of a wooden spoon into the hot oil; if it bubbles around it, the oil is hot enough. Drop 2 to 3 doughnuts at a time into the oil, taking care not to crowd the pot so it won't boil over. Deep-fry the doughnuts, turning them over halfway through, until golden, 2 to 3 minutes per side. Place on a wire rack to cool. Serve warm with My Mother's Chocolate Sauce drizzled over.

TIP: The doughnuts holes can be pierced and filled with jam after they've cooled.

MY MOTHER'S CHOCOLATE SAUCE

Makes 500ml / 2 cups

370g / 1¾ cups sugar	60g / ¾ cup cocoa powder	50g / 1.7 ounces 70% dark chocolate, broken into pieces
100ml / ⅓ cup plus 1 tablespoon light golden syrup (available at Amazon.com)	200ml / ¾ cup plus 1 tablespoon water	1 teaspoon vanilla paste
		¼ teaspoon sea salt

In a medium saucepan set over medium heat, combine all the ingredients. Whisk well and bring to a boil. Lower the heat and simmer, stirring occasionally, until luscious and glossy, 10 to 12 minutes.

Though it may not seem very thick at this point, the mixture will thicken as it cools. Sterilize a glass jar (see Tip, page 69) large enough to hold the sauce and with a wide opening to allow easy access to the sauce. Pour the chocolate sauce into the jar, and store in the fridge for up to 1 month. Serve cold or warm.

BLACKBERRY AND APPLE CRUMBLE

Serves 6

Little says comfort more than a freshly baked crumble drizzled with warm custard. You can use pretty much any seasonal fruit or berry—the possibilities are endless—but this is one version that I return to again and again. It freezes well; just leave it to cool before putting it in the freezer in an airtight container. Then you can have a dessert readily at hand when impromptu dinner guests swing by. Serve warm out of the oven with a scoop of vanilla ice cream or warm custard. To reheat a frozen crumble, simply pop it into a preheated oven at 100°C / 210°F and warm it gently, covered, for ten to twelve minutes. Uncover and increase the temperature to 180°C / 350°F. Bake another four to six minutes.

100g / 1 cup rolled oats

50g / ½ cup almond flour

125g / 1 cup all-purpose flour

130g / ⅔ cup packed light brown sugar

1 teaspoon ground cinnamon

Pinch of sea salt

170g / ¾ cup (1½ sticks) salted butter, cut into small pieces, room temperature

420g / 14 ounces Granny Smith apples, peeled, cored, and chopped

300g / 10 ounces blackberries

Preheat the oven to 180°C / 350°F.

In a large bowl, combine the oats, flours, sugar, cinnamon, and salt. Using your fingertips, rub the butter into the flour mixture until you have a soft, crumbly topping.

Place the apples and blackberries in a 25-centimeter / 10-inch pie dish, and cover with the crumble mixture.

Bake until the topping is golden brown, 25 to 30 minutes. Let cool slightly before serving.

SLOE GIN

Makes 1L / 4¼ cups

Per English tradition, each sloe (the fruit from a blackthorn plant) should be pierced a few times with a thorn from the bush. Impatient by nature, I use a sharp fork and pierce each sloe once. With their chalky dark-blue color, the berries look just as tart as they taste. Though they aren't very good eaten off the bush, with a bit of gin, sugar, and cinnamon, they are transformed. Sloe gin has the freshest flavor and a beautiful hue, as the berries change the color to velvet red. This is one of my all-time favorite late autumn drinks.

450g / 4½ cups sloes

200g / 1 cup caster sugar / superfine sugar

1 cinnamon stick, halved

1L / 4¼ cups quality gin (I like Conker Spirit or London Dry)

Pick the sloes after the first frost, or freeze your sloes picked at the end of the season overnight.

Prick each sloe with a sharp fork.

Sterilize (see Tip, page 69) two 500ml bottles (large enough to hold about 2¼ cups each). Divide the sloes between the bottles. Divide the sugar between the bottles and put half of the cinnamon stick in each bottle. Divide the gin between the bottles. Seal and store in a dark place. Shake once every day for 2 to 3 months. Strain through a fine-mesh sieve or cheesecloth before pouring back into sterilized bottles. Keep in a cool place for 2 to 3 months.

To serve, pour 1 part sloe gin to 5 parts tonic water into a glass. Serve chilled. This makes a lovely flavored gin to create a base for a very fresh-tasting gin and tonic. If you really enjoy gin, it can be served on its own in a small glass.

TIP: Try using the method described here but swap out the gin for your favorite whiskey, omitting the cinnamon stick.

MULLED CIDER

Makes 1L / 5 cups

When mulled cider shows up on the menu at the local pub, I get excited for the season ahead.

Wild autumnal storms may rage outside, but when I'm tucked up next to a roaring fire in my local pub with this drink in hand, I'm snug as can be. During autumn and winter, I often have a saucepan of mulled cider on low on the stove, ready to be ladled into mugs when friends stop by, or to enjoy after a wander in the woods with Mr. Whiskey. Needless to say, it also fills the cottage with a lovely aroma.

1L / 4¼ cups cloudy, dry apple cider

150ml / ½ cup ginger beer

Juice of 1 orange

Zest and juice of 1 unwaxed lemon

1 cinnamon stick, plus more for serving

4 whole cloves

Pinch of freshly grated nutmeg

1 orange, sliced, for serving

In a large saucepan set over low heat, combine the cider, ginger beer, orange juice, lemon zest and juice, 1 cinnamon stick, cloves, and nutmeg. Heat the mixture without letting it boil, about 15 minutes.

Serve ladled into glasses or mugs, with orange slices and a cinnamon stick in each.

MY MOTHER'S PLUM JAM

Makes 1.1L / 4²/₃ cups

This is a loose jam with a runnier consistency than non-Norwegians might be familiar with. The quality of the plums and the variety available will determine the deliciousness of the jam, so make sure to select the very best plums. Needless to say, when they are in season they have the most flavor, which will make your jam ever so tasty. Drizzle it on top of your breakfast porridge, on Norwegian Waffles (page 64), or on toast, and be sure to make some extra to give to friends and neighbors.

1kg / 2.2 pounds Victoria, Santa Rosa, or Burbank plums, pitted and halved

150ml / ½ cup plus 2 tablespoons water

1kg / 4¾ cups caster sugar / superfine sugar

Juice of 1 lemon

In a large saucepan set over medium heat, bring the plums and water to a simmer and cook until softened, 15 to 18 minutes. Stir in the sugar and lemon, and continue to cook until slightly thickened, 12 to 15 minutes.

Sterilize (see Tip, page 69) enough jars to hold the jam. Pour in the jam and tighten the lids. The jam will keep in a sterilized airtight jar in a dark cool place for up to 1 month or in the fridge after opening for up to 1 week.

*afternoon
tea*

There are few hours in life more agreeable than the hour
dedicated to the ceremony known as afternoon tea.

—HENRY JAMES

BEFORE I EVER SET FOOT on English soil, I was thoroughly entrenched in the art of enjoying a cup of something warm, like hot chocolate, during the colder months of the year. During summer, my mother would bring in freshly picked mint and let the herb soak in hot water. She'd pour the concoction into mugs, add a heaping spoonful of honey, and serve the tea to us as we sat next to each other in the kitchen, drifting in and out of heartfelt conversations. However, tea was a treat rather than a daily ritual.

On a chilly autumn day in October a few years back I ventured into the heart of the English countryside for the very first time. Arriving by train in the afternoon, tired and cold, I sought refuge in a tea room in the quaint village of Corfe Castle on the Isle of Purbeck. The windows were all steamed up from the many people seated around the tables, sipping their tea. The big fireplace in the middle of the room was hissing away energetically, and the clinking sound of spoons against porcelain cups was like a warm hum in the background.

"What can I bring you?" a server said, with her pen against a notepad, ready to scribble down my order as I took a seat at an empty table with a bench by the window. "Tea," I replied, glancing over at my neighboring table where cups, saucers, cutlery, teapots, and plates with jam and crumbs were all piled high, looking like quite the feast. "Afternoon tea?" she asked. Looking at the big clock on the wall by the door that showed it was just past four o'clock in the afternoon, I nodded and repeated, "Afternoon tea, please."

This was the beginning of something completely new to me, because what came out just a few minutes later, on a large tray, was a plate heaped with warm scones fresh out of the oven, jars of jam and what I later learned was clotted cream, and a big pot of tea with milk on the side. I wasn't sure what I'd just ordered, as I'd assumed my order of "afternoon tea" was simply a cup of tea enjoyed past noon. But to my delight, I now had an unexpected feast in front of me, so I smiled, said thank you, and glanced around the room to see if this was indeed what everyone else was eating, hoping to pick up tips on how to begin tucking in.

You'd think slathering half a scone with clotted cream and jam would be a straightforward process, much like buttering a slice of toast and then adding marmalade, but in this matter, England is divided. Some add the jam first and others add the clotted cream before covering it with a thick layer of jam. I didn't know about the controversy at the time and followed what I thought was the logical method of beginning with cream and ending with jam. Little did I know I'd chosen a side! Either way, this little treat is delicious however you enjoy it.

Legend has it that the Duchess of Bedford felt peckish in the hours that stretched between lunch and supper. She began asking for cakes to be served with her afternoon cup of tea, which of course quickly caught on, as it turned out she was not the only woman in high society with a rumbling tummy around four o'clock. Thus a ritual was born, one that I tumbled into that fateful October afternoon a few years back, a delicious ritual including tea, scones, cakes, and little finger sandwiches.

In Norway, we don't drink tea the way the English do, which always puzzles the people I meet here in the shire. "What do you drink with your scones?" they ask, wide-eyed and completely at a loss over what else one could drink with it. "We don't traditionally have scones in Norway," I say, matter-of-factly, which seems to further throw them for a loop. They then ask what we use as an edible vehicle for clotted cream. "We don't make clotted cream," I calmly reply, sending them over the edge with that last piece of information. The everyday rituals that we take for granted can seem oh-so-exciting for the foreigner, just as I was when I discovered afternoon tea. But I've since fallen head over heels with the whole concept and have adopted this daily routine

like it's my own. Like clockwork, at four on the dot my kettle whistles like an alarm clock, prompting me to take a break with a cuppa.

While afternoon tea may be an extravagant affair in places like the Ritz or the Wolseley in London—consisting of elegant sandwiches, towering cake stands with tempting little petit fours, individual cakes, and, of course, scones—in my cottage, it's a rather simple affair. I prepare a freshly brewed cup of my favorite tea blends, such as the traditional breakfast tea with milk, Earl Grey, and occasionally Lady Grey, both with milk, no sugar, and a humble cookie or two. With Mr. Whiskey resting at my feet, the kettle gives off a hiss on the stove, and I take a seat by the window, gazing out into the ever-changing seasonal landscape beyond my garden, and above the church spires in the distance.

It's perhaps these moments of solitude and calm that made me adopt this very English tradition so wholeheartedly. Every single day, as soon as steam rises from the kettle and my cup is filled, I switch off entirely, giving in to the nowness of being. It's a welcome break from the energetic rhythm of my daily life.

LEMON CURD SPONGE CAKE
WITH PISTACHIOS

Serves 4 to 6

This cake is decadent, and a lovely addition to a feast of an afternoon tea break. If you double the recipe, you get one glorious cake for a post-dinner sweet feast, but the recipe below, followed exactly as is, makes just enough for you and a handful of friends on a random afternoon. Its citrusy flavor and creamy consistency comes from lots of eggs, clotted cream, and that luscious lemon curd. I love to pair it with steaming hot Assam tea or Earl Grey, but if you'd like to make it more festive, serve with sparkling wine or a good bottle of prosecco. If you're unable to purchase or make clotted cream, you can substitute My Mother's Whipped Cream (page 125).

250g / 1⅓ cups salted butter, room temperature, plus more for greasing

200g / 1 cup caster sugar / superfine sugar

5 medium eggs

2 tablespoons whole milk

2 teaspoons vanilla paste

300g / 2⅓ cups self-rising flour

1 teaspoon baking powder

300g / 1½ cups Clotted Cream (page 124)

150ml / ½ cup plus 2 tablespoons Lemon Curd (page 69)

Zest of 1 unwaxed lemon

1 batch toasted pistachios (see Tip, page 125)

Icing sugar / confectioners' sugar, for sprinkling

Preheat the oven to 180°C / 350°F. Line the bottoms of two 12- to 15-centimeter / 5- to 6-inch round springform pans with parchment paper, with the edge of the paper extending past the base to allow for easy removal. Clip the sides of the pans shut and butter both the paper and the sides of the pans.

In a large bowl, beat the butter and sugar with an electric hand mixer until fluffy. Lightly beat the eggs in (don't be concerned if the mixture doesn't combine completely). Add the milk and vanilla paste, and beat until fluffy. Sift in the flour and baking powder, then carefully fold the ingredients together, making sure to keep the mixture airy. Divide the mixture evenly between the pans and smooth the surface with an offset spatula.

Bake until lightly golden, 15 to 20 minutes. Cover the pans with foil, and bake until a cake tester inserted in the middle of the cake comes out clean, about 20 minutes more. Let cool on a wire rack for 5 minutes, then remove the cakes from the pans and let cool completely on the rack.

To assemble, put one of the cake layers on a plate and spread the clotted cream over the top. Spread the lemon curd over the cream, then sprinkle half of the lemon zest and all the toasted pistachios over the curd. Place the second layer on top of the first, and sprinkle it with confectioners' sugar and the remaining lemon zest just before serving. I often cut the edges of the cake off, as I find they can harden through the baking process, but doing so is purely optional.

LISE'S CARROT CAKE

Serves 6 to 8

My oldest brother married a tall blond girl with big curly hair just when I'd lost my two front teeth. I'd gaze up at her in awe and admiration. She always treated me like her little sister, and I loved her from the moment we met. She and my brother both worked and studied in America for years, and, influenced by her time there, she brought back this recipe. It's a staple dessert at family gatherings, and we all fight over the last piece. It's a little bit about the actual cake, and a lot about the frosting.

CAKE

Salted butter, for greasing

400g / 2 cups packed dark brown sugar

4 medium eggs

250ml / 1 cup vegetable oil

220g / 1²/₃ cups all-purpose flour

2 teaspoons ground cinnamon

1 teaspoon baking powder

1 teaspoon sea salt

250g / 2 cups finely grated carrots

65g / ²/₃ cup roughly chopped walnuts (optional)

FROSTING

500g / 3³/₄ cups icing sugar / confectioners' sugar

100g / ½ cup cream cheese

100g / 7 tablespoons salted butter

2 teaspoons vanilla paste

50g / ½ cup roughly chopped walnuts (optional)

MAKE THE CAKE: Preheat the oven to 180°C / 350°F. Line two 20-centimeter / 8-inch round cake pans with parchment paper and butter the pans and paper.

In a large bowl, combine the brown sugar, eggs, and oil. Sift the flour, cinnamon, baking powder, and salt into the bowl. Stir well. Fold in the carrots and the walnuts, if using. Divide the batter between the prepared cake tins.

Bake until golden brown and a cake tester inserted in the center comes out clean, 35 to 40 minutes. Let cool to room temperature.

MAKE THE FROSTING: In a medium bowl, vigorously mix together the confectioners' sugar, cream cheese, butter, and vanilla paste until smooth.

ASSEMBLE THE CAKE: Place a layer of cake on a serving dish and spread half of the frosting evenly on top. Set the second layer on top and spread the remaining frosting on top. Sprinkle with the walnuts, if desired.

TANTE MARIE'S COFFEE AND FIG BREAD

Makes 2 small loaves

I never met Aunt Marie, or *Tante* Marie as we say in Norwegian. She was my grandmother's aunt. She moved to America in search of a new life at the tender age of eighteen. Embarking on this journey all by herself, sailing across the ocean to a new land, is nothing but awe-inspiring, and I wish I could've known her. Shortly after disembarking onto American soil, she met her future husband, a single father with six children, and together they had another six. What a woman! Aunt Marie was clearly strong and independent. It must run in the family, as my mother, grandmother, sister share the very same traits, and if I could invite anyone over for an afternoon tea, during which we while away the hours with conversations about life, I would have loved to have invited Tante Marie. Upon her first return to Norway for a visit after fifty years away, she gave this recipe to my mother, who had just married my father. Slathered with salted butter and warm, straight out of the oven, it's the perfect treat with tea or coffee. To make the bread caffeine-free, try Barleycup (or Pero), which works equally well and is the way my mother makes it.

Butter, for greasing and serving

550g / 4¼ cups all-purpose flour

3 teaspoons baking powder

1 teaspoon ground cinnamon

180ml / ¾ cup light golden syrup (available at Amazon.com)

180ml / ¾ cup strong espresso coffee

265g / 1½ cups finely chopped dried figs

235g / 1 cup plus 2 tablespoons sugar

1 teaspoon peeled, grated fresh ginger

Preheat the oven to 180°C / 350°F. Line 2 small loaf pans, 10 × 25 centimeters / 4 × 10 inches, with parchment paper. Butter the parchment.

In a large bowl, sift the flour, baking powder, and cinnamon. Add the syrup, coffee, figs, sugar, and ginger, and stir well. Pour the mixture evenly between the prepared pans.

Bake until browned and a cake tester inserted in the center comes out clean, 45 to 50 minutes. Serve toasted with butter.

LEMON AND HONEY POLENTA CAKE WITH PEACHES

Serves 6 to 8

During my time in Italy, I learned to cherish the humble polenta, and came to love its many delicious savory and sweet preparations. In my little English village, Pythouse Kitchen Garden, a walled garden with a charming café, often tempts me with their lemon polenta cake during afternoon tea. Back at the cottage, I've experimented with combinations of flavors. By adding peaches, lemon juice, and honey, this cake becomes ever so moist and full of flavor.

CAKE

225g / 1 cup (2 sticks) salted butter, room temperature, plus more for greasing

200g / 2 cups almond flour

125g / ¾ cup polenta

1 teaspoon baking powder

1 teaspoon vanilla paste

100g / ½ cup sugar

4 medium eggs

Zest and juice of 1½ unwaxed lemons

3 ripe peaches, pitted and sliced

1 tablespoon honey

TOPPING

125ml / ½ cup honey

Juice of 1 lemon

Preheat the oven to 180°C / 350°F. Line the base of a 22½-centimeter / 9-inch round springform cake pan with parchment paper, with the edge of the paper extending past the base to allow for easy removal of the cake. Clip the sides of the pan shut and butter the paper and the sides of the pan.

In a medium bowl, combine the almond flour, polenta, and baking powder.

In a large bowl, using an electric hand mixer, beat together the butter, vanilla paste, and sugar until creamy and fluffy, 3 to 5 minutes. Add the eggs one at a time, mixing after each addition. Using a flexible spatula, stir in the lemon zest and juice. Stir in the almond flour mixture. Pour the batter into the prepared cake pan and arrange the peach slices on top, side by side, completely covering the top. Drizzle with a tablespoon of honey.

Bake in the middle or lower rack in the oven until golden and a cake tester inserted in the center comes out clean, 55 to 60 minutes.

Meanwhile, make the topping: Combine the honey and lemon juice in a small bowl. Drizzle generously over the cake while it's still warm. Leave to soak for 5 to 10 minutes before serving warm.

NORWEGIAN COCONUT AND VANILLA ROLLS

SKOLEBRØD

Makes 10 rolls

I don't think there's a single little boy or a girl who grew up in Norway who doesn't know and cherish this baked treat. When autumn and winter storms tug viciously at the treetops outside, few things beat coming home from school, all tired and cold, to a crackling fireplace and warm *skolebrød*—which literally translates to "school bread"—waiting on the kitchen table alongside a steaming hot drink to rejuvenate you after a long day. I must admit, these rolls are best the day they're baked, and rarely do I buy them from a baker—they are always best homemade. As we say in Norwegian, *"her er det bare å kose seg,"* which means, "the only option you have here is to simply enjoy." And I hope you do.

570g / 4½ cups all-purpose flour, plus more for rolling

70g / ⅓ cup sugar

1 teaspoon finely ground cardamom

Pinch of sea salt

80g / 5½ tablespoons salted butter, plus more for greasing

250ml / 1 cup whole milk

2 tablespoons active dry yeast

2 medium eggs

Vanilla Cream (recipe follows)

Coconut Icing (recipe follows)

In a large bowl, combine the flour, sugar, cardamom, and salt.

In a small saucepan set over low heat, melt the butter. Add the milk and let warm, 5 to 8 minutes. Test the milk on the back of your hand; it's ready when it's the same temperature as your skin, about 37°C / 95°F. Remove the pan from the heat and gently whisk in the yeast. Let sit until slightly cooled, 2 to 3 minutes. Stir in 1 of the eggs. Pour the milk mixture into the flour mixture and stir until it's well combined and forms a dough. Transfer the dough to a floured surface, and knead until you have a smooth, elastic dough that springs back when touched, 10 to 12 minutes. (Feel free to use a stand mixer fitted with the dough hook for kneading. I prefer to use my hands, like my mother, but this

recipe continues

is just a matter of preference.) Place the dough back in the bowl, cover with a kitchen towel, and let rise in a warm place until doubled in size, 1½ to 2 hours.

Transfer the dough to a floured work surface and knead for 2 to 3 minutes. Butter a baking dish large enough to hold the rolls. Divide the dough into 10 equal pieces. Using your hands, roll each piece into a ball. Place the rolls on the baking dish with a little room between them for rising. Cover with a kitchen towel and let rise in a warm place until risen, about 45 minutes.

Preheat the oven to 170°C / 340°F.

Use your thumb to push a hole in the center of each roll. Fill each hole with 1 to 2 teaspoons of vanilla cream. Whisk the remaining egg and brush each roll with the egg wash, avoiding the vanilla cream area. Bake, checking on them halfway through, until the rolls are lightly golden, 10 to 12 minutes. Let cool on a wire rack. Once cool, spread the coconut icing and shredded coconut on each roll, again avoiding the vanilla area. Serve immediately.

VANILLA CREAM

Makes about ¼ cup

125ml / ½ cup whole milk	2 tablespoons sugar	1 teaspoon cornstarch
1½ tablespoons double cream / heavy cream	1 vanilla bean	1 medium egg yolk

In a small saucepan, combine the milk (hold back 1½ tablespoons), cream, and sugar. Cut the vanilla bean lengthways and scrape the seeds out with the back of a knife. Add the vanilla seeds and the empty pod to the milk mixture. Set the pan over medium-low heat and slowly bring the mixture to a simmer.

In a small bowl, whisk together the remaining 1½ tablespoons milk and the cornstarch until completely dissolved, then whisk in the egg yolk. Whisking constantly, slowly pour the warm milk mixture into the egg mixture in a thin stream, making sure not to scramble the eggs. Strain the mixture back into the saucepan through a fine-mesh sieve to get rid of any lumps. Bring to a simmer and cook, stirring, until thickened, 5 to 10 minutes (do not let it boil!). Pour the cream into a small bowl, cover, and let cool before using.

COCONUT ICING

Makes about 1 cup

100g / ¾ cup icing sugar / confectioners' sugar

4 teaspoons whole milk

4 tablespoons desiccated coconut

Sift the confectioners' sugar into a small bowl and add the milk. Mix well, until you have a smooth, lump-free frosting. Place the coconut in a separate small bowl. Use the back of a spoon to glaze a thin layer of icing on the sides of the rolls, avoiding the vanilla cream area. Dip the glazed parts of the rolls in the coconut.

ORANGE CINNAMON KNOTS

Makes 20 knots

As children we'd eat these cinnamon rolls straight out of the oven with a cold glass of milk upon returning home after school. However, these days I tend to add a bit of orange zest, twist them into knots, and enjoy them with my afternoon tea. They are definitely best eaten warm and on the day they are baked. Serve with a warm cup of citrusy Lady Grey tea or as a sweet treat for breakfast with a steaming hot cup of coffee.

DOUGH

570g / 4½ cups all-purpose flour, plus additional for rolling

1 teaspoon ground cardamom

70g / ⅓ cup granulated sugar

Pinch of sea salt

90g / 6 tablespoons salted butter, plus more for greasing

250ml / 1 cup whole milk

2 tablespoons active dry yeast

1 medium egg

CINNAMON FILLING

3½ tablespoons salted butter, room temperature

Zest of 2½ unwaxed oranges

1 tablespoon ground cinnamon

½ tablespoon ground cardamom

3 to 4 tablespoons dark brown sugar

1 medium egg, beaten, for brushing

Raw Demerara sugar, for garnish

MAKE THE DOUGH: In a large bowl, combine the flour, cardamom, granulated sugar, and salt.

In a small saucepan set over low heat, melt the butter. Add the milk and warm it until it is the same temperature as your skin, about 37°C / 95°F (test the milk on back of your hand). Remove the pan from the heat and gently whisk in the yeast. Let cool slightly for 2 to 3 minutes. Mix in the egg. Pour the milk mixture into the flour mixture and combine until you have a dough. Transfer the dough to a floured surface, and knead until the dough is elastic and springs back when touched, 10 to 12 minutes. (Feel free to use a stand mixer fitted with the dough hook for kneading. I prefer to use my hands, like my mother, but this is just a matter of preference.) Place the dough back in the bowl, cover with a kitchen towel, and let rise in a warm place until doubled in size, 1½ to 2 hours.

Butter a baking sheet that's large enough to hold the knots.

Put the dough onto a floured work surface and divide it in half. Using a rolling pin, roll out each half into a 15 × 50-centimeter / 6 × 20-inch rectangle.

PREPARE THE FILLING: In a small bowl, combine the butter, zest, cinnamon, cardamom, and brown sugar. Spread the mixture evenly over both rectangles. With the longest edge toward you, grab the corner nearest to you. Run your finger along a shorter edge until you reach the opposite corner, then fold the dough over and away from you, making a 7½ × 50-centimeter / 3 × 20-inch rectangle. Using a sharp knife, cut the dough into 5-centimeter / 2-inch-wide strips. Twist the strips, tie them into a knot, and place them on the prepared baking sheet. Cover with a kitchen towel and let rise in a warm place for 45 to 60 minutes.

Preheat the oven to 170°C / 340°F.

Brush the knots with the beaten egg and sprinkle Demerara sugar on top. Bake until lightly golden, 10 to 12 minutes. Let cool on wire racks for 5 minutes before enjoying warm.

ROSEWATER DROPS

ROSE SANDNØTTER

Makes 30 to 40 cookies

Gently perfumed like an English garden, these little cookies melt ever so gently on the tongue. Infused with a shy whiff of English rose, they are a delicate accompaniment for a warm cup of tea.

I adore these with Earl Grey, which feels a bit like a Mr. Tea meets Miss Rose. The consistency of the dough might feel unfamiliar as you work with it, due to the potato starch, but simply follow the recipe closely and you'll have a sweet treat ready for your afternoon tea in no time. These cookies keep well stored in an airtight container for up to a week, but I don't think any little drop will remain uneaten for that long.

125g / ⅔ cup salted butter, room temperature, plus more for greasing

130g / ⅔ cup caster sugar / superfine sugar

1 teaspoon vanilla paste

2 teaspoons rosewater

1 medium egg

60g / ½ cup all-purpose flour, plus more for rolling

250g / 1¾ cups potato starch

1 teaspoon baking powder

Preheat the oven to 180°C / 350°F with a rack set in the middle. Line a rimmed baking sheet with parchment paper and butter the paper.

In a large bowl, whisk together the butter, sugar, vanilla paste, and rosewater until light and fluffy, 2 to 3 minutes. Add the egg and whisk for another minute. Add the flour, potato starch, and baking powder, and stir well. Transfer the dough to a floured work surface and divide the dough in half. The dough should be quite soft and sticky. Gently roll the pieces out into 2 equally long sausages that are 2½ centimeters / 1 inch in diameter. Cut the sausages into 2-centimeter- / ¾-inch-thick disks and gently roll each disk in your hands into a ball. Place the balls on the prepared baking sheet, leaving room for them to rise. Press a fork into each ball to leave an imprint of the tines.

Bake in the middle oven rack until the cookies are light and porous, but not golden, 10 to 18 minutes. Let cool on a wire rack. The cookies will keep in an airtight container for up to 1 week.

ALMOND CELEBRATION WREATH

FEST KRANS

Makes 1 wreath

It's the glorious almond filling that makes this traditional Norwegian *fest krans*, or *kringle*, come alive. Serve it warm out of the oven with a generous sprinkle of frosting right as your friends arrive for tea. Its comforting warm aroma will fill your home with the most welcoming almond perfume, and is there truly anything more inviting than being greeted with freshly baked goods upon arrival in someone's home? Best enjoyed the day you bake it, the bread will also keep for a day or two in an airtight container.

DOUGH

80g / 5½ tablespoons salted butter, plus more for greasing

180ml / ¾ cup whole milk

25g / 2½ tablespoons active dry yeast

250g / 2 cups all-purpose flour, plus more for kneading

75g / ⅓ cup granulated sugar

1 teaspoon ground cardamom

Pinch of sea salt

1 medium egg, beaten, for brushing

1 to 2 tablespoons slivered almonds, for topping

ALMOND FILLING

50g / ⅓ cup almonds

1 medium egg white

55g / ¼ cup granulated sugar

FROSTING

1 medium egg white

185g / 1½ cups icing sugar / confectioners' sugar

¼ teaspoon fresh lemon juice

MAKE THE DOUGH: In a small saucepan set over low heat, melt the butter. Add the milk and heat until warm. Test the milk on the back of your hand; it's ready when it's the same temperature as your skin, about 37°C / 95°F. Add the yeast, stir gently to combine, and let sit until cooled slightly, 2 to 3 minutes.

In a large bowl, combine the flour, sugar, cardamom, and salt. Add the milk mixture and stir well. Transfer the dough to a floured work surface and knead until you have a smooth, elastic dough, 4 to 6 minutes. Place the dough back in the bowl and cover it with a kitchen towel. Let rise in a warm place until doubled in size, 30 to 45 minutes.

recipe continues

Preheat the oven to 200°C / 400°F with a rack set in the middle. Butter a rimmed baking sheet.

PREPARE THE FILLING: In a food processor, grind the almonds while adding the egg white and sugar until you have a paste-like consistency, 2 to 3 minutes.

Put the dough on a lightly floured work surface and knead the air out of the dough, 3 to 5 minutes. Shape the dough into a 50-centimeter- / 20-inch-long sausage. Using a rolling pin, roll the sausage out until it is 15 centimeters / 6 inches wide. Spread the almond paste evenly over it. Lift up a long end of the dough and roll it up into a log. Transfer the log to the prepared baking sheet, making sure the seam faces down, and turn the ends toward each other so they overlap, creating a circle. Brush with the beaten egg and sprinkle the almonds over the dough.

Bake in the middle of the oven until golden, 20 to 30 minutes. Let cool for 5 minutes on a wire rack.

MEANWHILE, MAKE THE FROSTING: In a medium bowl, whisk the egg white until a soft foam forms, 1 to 2 minutes. Whisk in the confectioners' sugar little by little until completely combined. Add the lemon juice and combine well. Set aside until the wreath is ready to be iced.

Once the cake has cooled a bit, simply ice the wreath by spooning over the icing in one single layer to cover the top.

MARIE'S BIRTHDAY CAKE

Serves 6 to 8

Being true to the traditional Norwegian *bløtekake*, a sponge cake with berries and whipped cream, this treat is usually served at birthdays and for special occasions. I've always stuck to this custom for the birthdays of friends, but after my mother and I visited our friends Mimi and Oddur Thorrison in their beautiful home in Medoc, France, Mimi inspired me to think outside the box. One day she served us wine-soaked strawberries with cream, and I thought back to my *bløtekake* recipe. Perhaps I should try soaking the strawberries in wine, ditch the apple juice traditionally used to soak the sponge cake, and instead employ the wine used for the strawberries? And thus this recipe was born. Serve with a glass of port wine. If I were to bake you one cake, and one cake only, this would be it.

BERRIES

600g / 3½ cups strawberries, sliced

½ bottle of your favorite red wine (I usually use Merlot or Malbec)

450g / 3⅔ cups raspberries

CAKE

Butter, for greasing

5 medium eggs

130g / ⅔ cup granulated sugar

1 teaspoon vanilla paste

100g / ⅔ cup all-purpose flour

1 teaspoon baking powder

Double batch Vanilla Cream (page 268)

1½ batches My Mother's Whipped Cream (page 125)

2 tablespoons icing sugar / confectioners' sugar, for decoration

PREPARE THE BERRIES: In a large bowl, soak 500g / 3 cups of strawberries in the red wine for 2 to 3 hours, covered, at room temperature. Keep the raspberries and the remaining strawberries fresh until the cake is ready to be assembled.

BAKE THE CAKES: Preheat the oven to 180°C / 350°F. Line the bottoms of two 24-centimeter / 9½-inch round springform cake pans with parchment paper, letting the edge of the paper extend past the base to allow for easy

recipe continues

removal of the cake. Clip the sides of the pans shut and butter both the paper and the sides of the pans.

In a medium bowl, beat the eggs, sugar, and vanilla paste until light and fluffy, 10 to 15 minutes. Sift in the flour and baking powder, and carefully fold the mixture together, making sure to keep it airy. Spoon the batter into the prepared pans.

Bake until lightly golden and a cake tester inserted in the center of the cake comes out clean, 20 to 25 minutes. Let cool for 5 to 10 minutes before removing from the pans. Let cool completely on a wire rack.

Select a tray or plate big enough to serve the cake on. Drain the strawberries, reserving the liquid. Place a layer of the sponge cake, bottom-side up, on the plate and gently drizzle half the liquid from the soaked strawberries to moisten the cake but not soak through. Using an offset spatula, spread half the vanilla cream over the cake, completely covering the whole surface right to the edge. Place half of the wine-soaked strawberries on top of the vanilla cream. Sprinkle on a third of the raspberries. Top with a third of the whipped cream. Add the second cake layer, bottom-side up. Repeat the layering process, then cover the top and sides with the remaining whipped cream. Decorate the top with the remaining fresh strawberries and raspberries. Sprinkle with confectioners' sugar.

PROSECCO SCONES

Makes 6 to 8 scones

This book would not be complete without a recipe for my favorite version of scones. The prosecco really does make a difference in making the scones ever so fluffy and sweet. My assistant for the cookbook, Abbie, used to get up early and make her favorite scones to serve when we hosted our cooking and photography workshops, and my versions evolved out of our kitchen conversations surrounding our love for this English tradition. These will keep in an airtight container for a few days, but I'm not sure you'll have any left by then. Serve warm and sliced in half, with Clotted Cream (page 124), Rosewater and Strawberry Jam (page 187), and your afternoon tea.

Butter, for greasing

350g / 2½ cups self-rising flour

55g / ¼ cup caster sugar / superfine sugar

1 teaspoon finely chopped fresh thyme

½ teaspoon sea salt

125ml / ½ cup double cream / heavy cream

125ml / ½ cup prosecco

2 tablespoons whole milk, for brushing

Clotted Cream (page 124), for serving

Jam, for serving

Preheat the oven to 220°C / 425°F. Lightly butter a large baking sheet.

Sift the flour into a medium bowl. Stir in the sugar, thyme, and salt. Pour in the cream and prosecco and stir to form a soft dough.

Turn the dough out onto a lightly floured work surface and knead lightly until combined, 1 to 2 minutes. Using a rolling pin, press the dough out to 1½-centimeters / ½-inch thick. Using a 7- to 8-centimeter / 3-inch round scone or biscuit cutter, cut out 6 to 8 scones. Place the scones on the prepared baking sheet and brush with milk. Reroll any scraps to make more scones.

Bake until lightly golden, 10 to 15 minutes.

To serve, layer the scones on a serving platter and place the clotted cream and jam in small bowls. Each person should take a scone and scoop clotted cream and jam onto their individual plate. To eat, break off a small, bite-size portion of your scone with your hands and, using a knife, slather the cream and jam onto the piece of scone.

ACKNOWLEDGMENTS

"The first thing you did when you entered this world was to smile," my mother reminds me when I ask about my birth. "The nurses were all gathered around looking at you smiling from your little crib."

"How could I not have smiled," I reply, "with you as my mother to guide me and love me through life."

Words cannot begin to describe the gratitude I feel toward my parents. Thank you for loving me unconditionally, for tirelessly supporting me, for including me in every conversation, for listening to my many, many ideas, for teaching me how to grow wings, but most important, for staying true to who you are, what you believe, and for choosing to stay together and never giving up on me, on us as a family, or on each other. You two are my lighthouse.

Thank you, to my oldest brother, Øyvind, to my sister, Ingunn, and to my brother Simen, for being my friends, my constant support, for never giving up on me, for being so quick to forgive, and for inspiring me with how you live your lives. I love you.

The two musketeers, Hans Arne Fagertun and Runar Strand: you two are truly medicine, and I cherish your unconditional friendship.

To the Hole family, for opening your hearts and home to me, and for your generous friendship.

To my editor, Charlie Brotherstone, for all the encouragement and help on guiding me through the process of making this book.

To my editors for the book, Ashley Meyer, for believing I had a book in me and for encouraging me every step of the way, and to Raquel Pelzel for being willing to take on the book mid journey and skillfully guiding me toward publication. And to Andrea Portanova, for all your help in navigating the in-betweens. To Doris Cooper, for trusting and believing in me on this book journey, and to Marysarah Quinn for designing the book and bringing it all to life.

To my assistant, Abbie Melle, without whose patience, assistance, and goodness this book wouldn't have been the same.

Heather Whitehead, whose friendship and gloriously inspiring madness feels like a harbor of love and encouragement.

Alexis Delaney, for your inspiring vision on food and for sharing your recipe with me.

To all the incredible recipe testers who have generously given of their time to help make the recipes in this book their very best.

Maria Villmones Bodenson, for all your help and encouragement.

Tracey Wood, Lindsay Radclyffe, Brittany Kiel, Bettina Ruegge, Siri Rolness, Ashlyn Holmes, Erin Prelypchan, Dinusha Jayatillake, Coolier Lumpkin, Amanda Barnes, Donna Gutierrez, Megham Kirk, Julie Simon, Helen Pockett, Adana Celik, Joanne Spittler, Sarah Hemsley, Chris Rogers, Angela Hade Harris, Luisa Koller, Naomi Kooijmans, Sally Boyle, Peggy Hoeben, Robyn Thompson, Marta Karcz, Jill Haapaniemi, Ashima Singhal, Kaitlyn Hale, Jordan Depina, Anna Hansson, Johanna Furuhjelm, Christine Haerra, Natasha Seidel, Dorota Dudek-Thien, and Sif Orellana.

INDEX

Note: Page references in *italics* indicate photographs.